WRITING FOR RADIO

A Practical Guide

WRITING FOR RADIO

A Practical Guide

Annie Caulfield

THE CROWOOD PRESS

First published in 2009 by
The Crowood Press Ltd
Ramsbury, Marlborough
Wiltshire SN8 2HR

www.crowood.com

British Library Cataloguing-in-Publication Data
A catalogue record for this book is available from the British Library.

ISBN 978 1 84797 095 4

Typeset by S.R. Nova Pvt Ltd., Bangalore, India

Printed and bound in Spain by Graphy Cems

CONTENTS

INTRODUCTION

There's a cliché about radio drama I've heard more times than even a cliché should be heard: 'I like radio, the pictures are better.' I understand what this means; I just don't think it's right. It isn't fair to radio to make it compete with visual media; it is equal, but different. It doesn't need to make excuses for itself by pretending to have the attributes of other forms.

With the special intimate quality of radio we return, however technologically complex the production, to the human voice telling us a story. We remember how evocative sounds, isolated or in composition, can be for us. We are reminded how much power there can be in a single word.

> The difference between the right word and the nearly right word is the same as that between lightning and the lightning bug.
>
> Mark Twain

This book aims to be of interest to curious radio listeners as well as writers. It is written with passion as well as expertise gleaned from producers, writers, directors and technicians far more experienced than myself. Writing for radio documentary, soaps, panel shows and comedy are all addressed in this book, but the main topic is writing radio drama. Most of the suggestions about how to write successful radio drama apply to speech radio in general.

> People love stories, and there is no better or more intimate medium for the telling of stories than radio. A good radio drama feels like it is being performed for you and you alone. There is no sense of sitting down to share a dramatic experience that you get when going to the cinema or theatre. The radio drama experience is one where you eavesdrop, alone, to a drama playing out on the airwaves, and when the story is strong and the characters compelling, there is no more powerful medium in the world.
>
> But of course we can never take radio drama for granted; in radio terms drama is expensive, and in many countries it has already withered and died. But in Britain, with its strong dramatic tradition, and the realization that the medium is a breeding ground for writers and actors, radio drama will survive, I trust, as long as radio exists as a medium.
>
> Gordon House, Former Head of BBC World Service Drama

1 WHY WRITE A RADIO PLAY?

A television producer once told me that I was wasting my time writing radio drama. They described it as 'a sideshow of a sideshow'.

Radio drama may not pay dizzying sums, or bring immediate fame and glittering prizes. It might bring a line in the *Radio Times* rather than a name in lights, but for writers, radio is a place where they are treated as being at least as important as the studio runner; they can be involved in the process from start to finish and they can have a production realized that comes very close to the production they imagined.

Radio has been a way in to a career as a dramatist for many successful writers and is revisited by just as many who are far above the sideshow level of their careers. Tom Stoppard, Edward Bond, Howard Barker, Anthony Minghella, Peter Barnes, Roy Williams, Sarah Daniels, Mark Ravenhill, Lee Hall – there's a very long list of contemporary writers who don't think radio is too obscure or old hat, who choose to revisit to the medium's special qualities.

> The limits on radio drama are those we put on it ourselves: habit, low expectations, our preference for the familiar and, well, the usual shortage of genius.
>
> John Taylor, Creative Director, Fiction Factory Productions

RADIO DRAMA – BIGGER THAN YOU'D THINK

This book is intended to inspire and encourage people to begin their writing careers in radio. They may already be writing and need to branch out, perhaps taking a rest from the treadmill of television series writing and wanting to try something where the writer has more freedom from interference. Or perhaps the writer is considering the different possibilities available in radio drama compared with stage drama.

With the exception of those few writers who attract massive Broadway or West End audiences, a stage play will not achieve the audience figures of a radio play. The average audience figure for a BBC radio afternoon play in 2008 was 600,000. Your first play on at the Royal Court or the Cottesloe couldn't achieve these figures in a month of performances. It wouldn't be physically possible, no matter how crammed the theatre was every night. A first radio play has this ready-made audience of over half a million people.

If a novel sold over half a million copies the publishers would be buying the author lavish lunches and marking them out as a rising star. A radio dramatist can achieve a massive audience and no one will know their name; except the listeners they touched with their writing, of course – those hundreds and thousands of listeners.

Radio may not be a high profile writing form, but it's far from being a sideshow.

INTERNATIONAL AUDIENCES

A radio play will go out all over the world; what the writer wants listeners to think and feel is not restricted to those with the price of a ticket. Audiences in the furthest locations can pick up British radio through the internet; they can listen through internet repeat facilities at a time to suit themselves. With battery power and wind-up portables, radio can go where electricity runs out and television satellite signals are blocked. Many successful radio plays are sold in boxed set recordings so their life goes on and on.

AUDIENCE REACTION

A good radio play does not go unnoticed by the people it is really for, the listeners. There is no heady moment of applause at the curtain call; but then again, the writer is spared the agony of watching a first night audience for a flicker of the right reaction on their faces. There are reviews and previews in national papers, but the writer doesn't have to suffer the tension of a theatre press night. A bad review for a radio play is distressing, a bad mark for the writer, but it won't make or break the production; the play has already been broadcast, or is scheduled for broadcast. Reviews and previews for radio drama tend to be tucked away at the back of the television section, so the audience is more likely to make up their minds to listen based on the subject matter, the lead actor, recognizing the writer's name or, most importantly, the first few minutes of the broadcast.

Radio drama can never compete with film and television for audience numbers. Yet a good radio play won't fail to find a distributor, or be dropped because of changes in management at the station. Once a radio play has been commissioned, the writer can rest content that it will reach the audience. There are rare exceptions to this that I'll explain later but a radio play seldom gets commissioned only to sink without a trace.

Radio drama sometimes hits the doldrums. The plays become safe and the audience as predictable as the customers for different types of daily news papers. There are loyal listeners and there are those who would never listen to radio drama any more than they'd buy a broadsheet newspaper. At times like these, writers avoid the medium because they see it as being too staid, too cosy – and not a proper home for their shocking truths or unnerving jokes. They take their ideas elsewhere and their audience isn't tempted to try radio. Then a new wave of producers and writers comes in and battles are fought to change the audience profile.

New Audiences

It is unlikely that seventeen-year-olds will suddenly be attracted to radio drama in droves; they have far better things to do – although students do listen, particularly to comedy. But older listeners, who may previously have felt excluded because of race, sexuality or range of interests, or possibly have just been bored, might be tempted by changes in the radio drama output to begin listening, or return to listening, and spread the word. For example, Radio 3, perceived home of classical music, serious arts documentaries and classical drama, recently produced a play by Caryl Phillips about soul singer Marvin Gaye – a new direction, attracting new listeners.

For some of the audience, a radio drama may be their last link with a world they can't access because of failing health, or because they live in a remote or dangerous place. Conversely a radio drama may open the eyes of the thriving and comfortable to events and emotions they never imagined would bother them.

The Power of Sound

It's unusual to walk through even the smallest of towns without hearing music playing, talk radio blaring, dogs barking, traffic roaring by (or grunting through a snarl-up), not to mention umpteen overheard conversations. Unless we wear very powerful headphones, we can't shut sound out. There's no equivalent of closing our eyes to keep it all out.

Sounds can be overwhelming – a helicopter overhead, party music next door, a verbose fellow passenger on the train – we talk about unwanted noise driving us mad. We like to choose what we hear, so if the sound is too loud, grating or unavoidable, it becomes a torment. We talk about noise making us feel that we can't think straight.

In order to think straight we might, after a difficult day, put on music we love, or seek out quiet. Sound, we know already, can trouble or soothe our thoughts. Sound can overwhelm our emotions. Writing for radio means taking a very powerful route into a listener's emotional life.

The actor is talking right into the microphone. The listener may be inches away from the radio speakers. There's an extraordinary intimacy in radio.

Anne Edyvean, BBC drama producer

WHO IS LISTENING?

There are outbursts of market research at BBC radio. Figures show that the average listener to radio drama is over forty and educated. There is a high proportion of female listeners and retired people. There is, however, no reason why the dramas should only reflect the world the listeners inhabit. Part of the reason for listening is to learn something, to feel involved in worlds unvisited; to empathize with situations we haven't experienced, but nevertheless could, one day.

So many times I have heard someone say, 'I heard a really interesting radio play this week.' And they go on to describe something that I know is outside their world. They have overheard another world, had an aspect of the past illuminated or been forced to stretch their mind to imagined futures. People seldom say, 'I heard a radio play today. It was so interesting because it was about someone exactly like me.'

It may depend how interesting the listener is I suppose.

Listeners are more likely to recognize situations and emotions, and to be interested to hear how someone very different copes, triumphs or fails in that situation. It is never a good idea to try to pre-empt the nature of the audience for a radio drama. A listener may be someone who is completely outside the demographic, just flicking along the dial – your play may have surprised them by appealing to them and a convert has been made. Or they may be a habitual listener, somewhat tired of the plays about educated female retired people, and relish an insight into Northern Soul, Eritrean freedom fighters or Icelandic teenage angst.

It is better to imagine drawing an audience. Find a subject and style of writing that will attract attention. Think of ways to hold their attention – some techniques for this will be explained in this book, but an individual vision, an urgency and energy in the writing are essential. Even habitual listeners can turn off and they are never as easy to second guess as market research might suggest. Educated people over forty are all very, very different. Female listeners do not want to hear domestic dramas all the time, any more than older listeners lack any curiosity about the world that teenagers live in today.

I can do all kinds of other things while I listen to radio drama, and I don't have to share the listening experience with anyone else if I don't want to. I can devise my own scenery, and draw the faces of the characters.

Marilyn Imrie, independent drama producer

THE UNEXPECTED AUDIENCE

Radios run on mains electricity, batteries or by a clockwork mechanism. Radio can be heard through digital television, car stereos or on the internet. Listeners could be in the garden or in a factory; they could be in a desert or a jungle. The portability of radio means the audience is more unpredictable than that of a theatre or cinema audience. Listeners want the radio with them for company, for distraction, or for information – but they have seldom made a commitment to listen. A radio audience is all over the place, listening in all sorts of ways but is easily distracted.

Online radio stations are proliferating, there are more and more independent broadcast stations and the pirate stations run from teenagers' bedrooms are ever present. Radio is a difficult medium to suppress. It can reach beyond electricity and beyond boundaries. This is exciting – but wherever they are, the listener can still wander off or switch off.

It can be mind-boggling to think how far away a radio audience might be. It is also mind-boggling to think how the audience might differ in culture, age, ethnicity, experience and education. Trying to second guess where the audience is, what they might be doing and who they might be is a problem for market researchers, not writers. A writer writes to express something in themself; if they've expressed it well, then it communicates. Who the writer communicates with is unknowable. Arthur Miller said that he felt he was casting his bread upon the waters when he wrote a play. With radio drama the waters are broad.

Occasionally, as if a message in a bottle has been returned, the reaction of a listener rather than a critic, can come back to astonish the writer. The BBC World Service soap opera *Westway* had audiences of up to thirty-five million for its fifteen-minute dramas about West London doctors. These listeners were in Africa, India and America. Fan mail came in from workers in remote power stations in China and truck drivers in Seattle. Then there was a heart-rending email from a group of women in Taliban-ruled Afghanistan who listened to the programmes in secret meetings.

Some World Service listeners had complained about *Westway* when it first went on air, feeling that the BBC World Service was no place for something as trivial as a soap opera. For the women in Afghanistan, *Westway* was profoundly important; it reminded them of a world were women were doctors, drivers, nurses, householders – and all able to speak their minds. It was far from trivial to them.

Who is listening? You never know.

WHEN NOT TO WRITE A RADIO PLAY

If you have a very visual imagination perhaps film and television would be better for you as a writer. If you like in-depth analysis of ideas rather than glancing insights, then your imagination might be better suited to prose. The key to radio drama is the dialogue; if you don't relish the way people speak and notice the words left unsaid in their sentences, then this may not be the best place to begin writing.

If you concentrate on facts about radio demographics and scan statistics of successful radio plays of the past, then you might be going about things the wrong way. The most important thing is to tell the story you want to tell, knowing that in your own mind you can hear voices telling it. It could be twenty voices or just one. Capturing how those voices sound is more important than knowing a great deal about the technicalities of radio production and commissioning processes.

Technicalities and script layout will be addressed in this book but are not as troublesome as first-time writers might imagine. If the writer listens to radio, glances at some typical scripts and uses their common sense, their talent will out. However, it may not come out if it isn't there. Just as someone can have all the music lessons time allows and the best guitar in the world, it won't make them Eric Clapton. Then again, no one knows if they're Clapton till they try, and it helps the audience appreciate you if you've learnt to play recognizable notes.

IS ANYONE GOING TO LISTEN?

In normal circumstances, radio has the advantage that it doesn't dominate the listener's attention. They can drive, baby-sit, cook, build a shed and go jogging while listening to the radio. Radio is company through dull chores or lonely tasks, while not stopping the listener doing what needs to be done. Any situation where a person can do something while having a conversation at the same time is a situation where they could be listening to the radio.

The writer's aim, of course, is to stop them in their tracks, preferably without causing a traffic pile-up or a dropped infant. A piece of radio has really succeeded when the listener forgets the task in hand and only listens. In the meantime, its portability and its lack of demand on the attention, compared to television or a book, is what will attract listeners to radio in the first instance.

WHO IS MAKING THE PLAYS?

There are changes in the air. Channel 4 Television is moving in to radio and plans to move into drama. They promise to create the kind of upheaval in expectations of radio that they created in television. They plan to create radio drama that is appealing to younger audiences; tackling more disturbing subjects and experimenting with technique. All this is at the drawing board stage as this book goes to print.

Hopefully Channel 4 will introduce a larger element of competition to the field of radio drama, encouraging existing producers to be more innovative and daring. It's hoped Channel 4 will do more to generate publicity and curiosity about radio dramas. At the very least, it will provide another place for writers to go with their scripts.

Some commercial stations try scripted sketch shows. Student and amateur radio dramas are on the internet, paving the way for all kinds of experiment and unregulated output. There is no reason why you couldn't create your own short radio drama and put it on the internet; this is easier than putting videos on *Youtube* and is a good calling card. Radio advertisements are often presented as tiny dramas – not Shakespeare, but a way to make a living in radio and learn to be concise. At present, however, the powerhouse for radio drama production in Britain is the BBC. They have the licence fee funding to pay for it and they have worldwide broadcast networks. It is rare for technicians, actors, directors or writers to learn about radio drama somewhere other than the BBC.

Competition is healthy, but if profit were the only incentive for radio drama production, would there be so many chances given to the completely inexperienced as are given in the BBC's subsidized environment? Currently over twenty per cent of BBC radio drama commissions go to writers new to radio. There is no radio equivalent of the studio or upstairs theatre, where beginners are tucked away to try their early works. In radio, beginners are put on the air alongside well-established writers. Without the testing ground of publicly funded radio, writers could be left with fringe theatre and occasional incentives in film and television to open the doors for them.

The only way to really learn to write any form of drama is in production. Until that happens, the writer has a musical score and no musical instruments. More than any other outlet, BBC radio is there, waiting to help the new writer learn how to work with all the other components that make up a good drama. The BBC is currently the home of radio drama but who else could be trusted to keep the house in order? Who else would have the economic liberty to look for innovation, quality and integrity in the radio output rather than commercial viability? Most commercial speech radio stations resort to the chat show or phone-in format because they are so much cheaper than drama production.

That said, it can be a huge pain when your play, or your idea for a radio play is turned down by the BBC. There's little else to do but go away and come back with something new. Compared to television and film, however, the chances that you will break through eventually in radio are hugely favourable. The BBC has hours and hours of radio drama airtime to fill with original work – hundreds of hours. Theatre, film and television don't have nearly the same amount of time available, or the money to take the risk on your early attempts to be a dramatist. More outlets would be great, but whatever its shortcomings, the BBC drama department's public funding provides a generous starting point for technicians, producers, directors and actors, as well as writers.

AND YET MORE ADVANTAGES FOR RADIO WRITERS...

I like the fact that the whole process from final draft to delivery is so quick. And the director has so much input into the drafts up to the final one. I like that momentum. It makes for instant and instinctive choices which often don't get in other media.

Marina Caldarone, independent director/producer

In radio, if you have a play commissioned, you can rest comfortably in the knowledge that once written it will be recorded and broadcast. Only exceptional events will prevent this happening. Even if you have made a terrible mess of the script, the producer will help you get it right rather than abandon the project.

In television, all manner of whims, regime changes and panics over the script can result in your commission being dropped. As there's so much money and kudos at stake, everyone is terrified of making a mistake. It is far easier to say 'no' than 'yes'. A pilot of your television script may even be recorded but never broadcast. In film, the chances of getting from script commission to the local multiplex are even slimmer. The more money involved, the more cautious people are about committing themselves to the next step.

In radio there isn't a team of script editors, under-producers, passing-through-producers, executive and senior producers interfering with your script. You work with one person from start to finish. The radio producer is also the script editor, is usually the director and supervises the final edit. Occasionally a director may be brought in to do the recording if you have a very busy producer or a producer suddenly taken ill, but at this stage there won't be a new voice giving opinions on the fundamentals of the script. For any writer who has worked in film or television, the clarity of this through-line is a joy. Eventually you will get your play out into the world, fairly close to the play you intended at the beginning.

In theatre, with a new play it is often possible to lose focus through a long rehearsal period. The writer can lose a sense of the play they intended. Financial constraints can limit the worlds it is possible to create on stage. Fast movement from atmosphere to atmosphere isn't easy. In theatre, gaining access to a character's inner thoughts requires devices such as the soliloquy, that are not as intimate as the eavesdropping that can be done in radio. In radio, very simple shifts are required to go from internal to external.

Similarly, theatre needs scene changes or stylized indicators to show movement through time. The shift from past to present in radio drama may only need the slightest of sound effects.

ACTORS

Television and film can be very performer-led. Despite all the generous remarks movie stars make about the importance of a good script, it is the presence of the movie star that will have got the film made.

Often in television we'll hear that the broadcasters are looking for a good vehicle for a star who's leaving a soap opera. Their acting ability may kill your script but in order to get it made, you have to let your script become a vehicle and not necessarily the drama you intended at all. If anyone cares what you intended by the time the cameras are recording, you'd be very lucky indeed.

In radio, the compromises demanded are few. Expressing the script is what matters in fact as well as sentiment. The writer is still allowed to call the tune.

In theatre, unless you are going into a very prestigious venue, it isn't easy to get the cast you want. On radio, a first-time writer can ask for a dream cast and often get it. Writers are around on recording day. Although the broadcast is the public performance, the recording feels more like the first night for the writer – this is when their play comes to life, although usually there's still some work to be done. Sometimes urgent rewrites are required; sometimes the writer is grateful for an eleventh-hour chance to tweak a scene.

Radio actors generally like having the writer around throughout the recording day. They can ask questions and the writer can explain if he thinks a line's been misunderstood. Actors can help an inexperienced writer a great deal; noticing why they find a line unsayable, or a scene confusing, can be an invaluable lesson.

Actors love radio drama – no lines to learn and they're in and out in a couple of days. Actors famous for one type of role may find radio the only place left where they can play against their typecasting. The very small publicity spotlight shone on a radio play can mean that an actor is happier to take a risk playing an unusual role.

> Radio's great, you can wear whatever's lying on the bedroom chair and you don't have to shave.
>
> Lenny Henry, comedian and actor

WHAT CAN GO WRONG?

Exceptional events might intervene. I delivered a play about architects working for Saddam Hussein the day Iraq was invaded. The play had to be dropped. Perhaps, when we're all old and grey, it can resurface as a piece of history.

Producers are increasingly aware of the dangers of litigation. They have the expertise of the BBC legal department to turn to for advice, so that the writer need not panic about what is legal and what isn't. If you are saying something libellous about a living rock star then it's unlikely the play will be made – although if you have copious proof of wrongdoing by said rock star and exposing the story is in the public interest, you may be backed to the hilt.

If your rock star has died, there are considerations to be made regarding living family members; they should at least be warned that the play is going out and may even want to issue statements in the press condemning your work. Again, it is unusual for a play to get to the stage of being recorded without proper inquiries being made.

I was once commissioned to write a play about a political campaigner who was still living. She refused to give permission for any dramatization of her life. However, the producer and commissioner deemed the campaigner's political movement was as important as its leader. They felt it was a subject still worth exploring and suggested solutions. I was able to use news archive recordings of the leader's actual speeches, as these were in the public domain. I created a fictional member of the political movement and told her story, with her comments on the actions of the leader. In the end the fictional route gave me more freedom and a broader take on the story.

LISTEN TO THE NOBODY

The thoughts of a great man's servant on the eve of a crisis often make better radio drama than the thoughts of a great man. The lesser character can be irreverent, observant and a bridge to greatness for us lesser mortals listening in. It also avoids criticism from pedants who might write in saying, 'But Napoleon never thought much of Blucher, it's recorded in his letter to so and so.' But Napoleon's footman's thoughts on Blucher? Who knows; who cares? Except the radio dramatist.

A film about the battle of Waterloo, with Napoleon as the man of action, will work far better than a radio drama about Waterloo because cinema has scale. Radio, however, has intimacy; it is the natural medium for behind-the-scenes, below-stairs conversations. An imagined servant belongs to the writer whereas Napoleon belongs to history.

If in doubt, invent a character to speak your words and do the things you need doing. If there are recordings available, then let the historical or famous figure speak for themself. If their speeches and actions are on public record, no one can complain you've misrepresented them. However, if you put words into their mouths and speculate on a secret, unrecorded life, you could face litigation or a barrage of criticism that would muddy appreciation of your play and obscure the story you wanted to tell.

WHAT ELSE CAN GO WRONG?

Large bestselling books are written about the terrible things done to innocent screenwriters. Perhaps unfortunately for my hopes of a bestseller, there are few persistent cruelties to writers of radio drama. Except perhaps the paltry fees. If you are determined to write only to be rich, your life will go very wrong in radio. To be creatively fulfilled, however, radio isn't a bad place to start or to seek refuge in.

In normal circumstances radio producers are very dedicated to writers; they help you learn on the job and won't drop a play because they think the script needs a lot of work. Perhaps you are certain that the script is exactly as it should be. It's up to the producer to prove their case for change, although they could refuse to record it. This would be a terrible and unusual impasse to reach, but at least in radio you are only fighting one person, not some huge television script department.

It may be that having fought the producer round to your way of thinking, you get to the studio and the great star chosen for the lead is terrible or, as I did hear tell of once, drunk. A good producer-director can only try their best to cajole a decent performance out of the star. Later, in the editing suite their part may have to be shaved to a minimum. If the performance is an irretrievable disaster it's not impossible for the play to be recorded with a new cast. If the commissioner liked the script and wanted it for broadcast at a particular time then the writer and producer can talk them into allowing a second recording. It is nothing like the disastrous experience involved in reshooting a film, or the horror of watching someone mess up your lines for the entire run of a stage play.

If your star pulls out at the eleventh hour and a substitute 'ordinary' actor has to be phoned at the crack of dawn on recording day, the show will still go on. The substitute doesn't have to learn lines; the existence of the play doesn't depend on its being a vehicle for the star.

If the head of radio drama changes, projects in the pipeline are very seldom abandoned by the new broom of a new regime the way they are in television and film. Working with small budgets, with a large number of drama slots to be filled, radio is not a wasteful medium.

Of course radio is full of ego and backstabbing internal politics – human beings work there. But there is more sense of people being there to get work done than working their way to a position of power. Those after power in the media are soon gone to television and film. Radio remains in the hands of people who want to make good work.

So what can go wrong? People could stop listening to the radio, or at least stop listening to speech radio. Yet film, television, CDs, Gameboys, Wii, DVD, Blueray, digital downloads and all the ever-burgeoning new technologies haven't killed radio. There are more stations; there is better sound quality and there are constant attempts to address the changing nature of the audience with different language stations, cultural content and voices from different English-speaking regions. People could stop listening to the radio. The sky might fall.

Or, potential radio writers could spend too much time reading theory, anecdote and opinion and get no help with the actual writing, so let's move on to that. Plenty more theory later.

2 WHERE TO START?

To write for radio, the best starting point is to listen to as much radio drama as possible. Some of it may not be good or may not be about anything of interest to you. The main thing is to start hearing how plays work. The strong ones will stand out. Why?

Think about this 'why?' Perhaps the answer that you've come up with will be proved correct in the next radio play you hear. The bad play did such-and-such, whereas the good play is clearly doing such-and-such. Perhaps you won't be able to pin down the answer exactly, but you'll be learning nonetheless by a process of osmosis.

Just because you hope to become a radio dramatist, there's no need to lie down in a darkened room to listen to radio plays. Or to sit listening while tensed at your desk with a notebook. It is probably better to listen as if you were an ordinary listener – driving, washing the dog, cooking the dinner – doing something else at the same time. Wait and see what makes you stop in your tracks.

Listen and think about your own ideas. If you have a head full of stories, would this be the way to tell them? Think in detail about one of your stories. Imagine how it would sound on radio. This might be the moment to close your eyes. What would be the first thing the listener would hear?

TELLING TALES

> All radio plays really need to be detective stories.
>
> Jeremy Mortimer, senior BBC drama producer

The first step in writing radio drama is to think about how we deal with sound in our lives. We hear something and think, 'What's that?' Then we either recognize the sound, or we don't. If we recognize it, for example, as a car door opening and closing, we then have a new question – 'Who is getting out of the car?' If we don't recognize the sound we think, 'That's weird, what *is* that?' Perhaps we go to look, but if we can't, we listen harder, hoping to recognize the sound on second hearing. Or we wait for dialogue to give us clues.

In radio drama, as in life, we hear something and want to know what it is. Already our ears are leading us in to a detective story. What we hear in the first few moments of the drama should begin the story, not just set the scene. From that point, the questions should start. We have to make people ask – what, who, where, why?

So, someone has got out of a car; how do we tell people who they are? Perhaps we then introduce a second character who says, 'Hello, Jane.' This doesn't help us at all. It tells us nothing about Jane and nothing about the speaker.

The speaker could say, 'Hello, Mother.' This is more helpful. But perhaps we need to use this opening line to do more. What if the speaker says: 'Mother, you're always late these days'? Then we're getting somewhere with the story. Is Mother up to something? Having problems? Has Mother decided that she's sick and tired of the speaker and is deliberately inconveniencing her?

Within the first line the detective story begins. We want to find out about these people and what they're up to. There may be no corpse in the library nor a bullion train robbed, but the listener should want to solve the mysteries about these people who have appeared in the airwaves all the same.

Building the First Scene

So, someone gets out of a car. It's mother, who, the first speaker, let's call her Linda, tells us is always late these days. There may be clues in the voices to tell us more about these characters – their age, race, class and attitude to each other. In one line, huge amounts of information can be communicated. It is more important to make sure there are still questions left to be asked.

If Linda said, 'Oh Mother, since we moved from Yorkshire and you took up gambling, you're always late and it's very inconvenient for me as you know I need you to look after the children when I'm at work,' this would be hopeless. We know too much of the story already. And the things we know are not that interesting. The information doesn't make us think: 'What's happening here, I need to know more.'

Perhaps if Linda said, 'Oh Mother, you're always late these days, you know I've no one else to help me,' then there's something to ask about. No one else to help Linda do what? Why hasn't she anyone else? And why is Mother acting up?

Establishing Character

Of course, one of the questions the listener will ask is, 'Do I like this character? Do I trust them?' Like Columbo at a murder scene, the listener needs to accumulate facts but also to form an impression of the suspects. Even in the most minimalist or amoral drama, we need to know whose side we're on.

We may be misled and find we're on the side of the murderer, the gambler, the liar, the coward or the bore. This doesn't matter if we've wanted to know what happens to them from the minute the play begins. We can switch allegiance later in the play, but to begin with we're following someone who has captured our curiosity. Even if we decide quite quickly that the character is vile, we might then be curious to see if they get their comeuppance. Even if we start confident that we know whose side we're on, then switch emotional allegiance, we are still following the story of the character we were drawn to first.

So at any moment the listener could decide they don't like Linda. At any moment they could take against the mother. They could dislike both characters. This isn't necessarily important. What we need to ensure is that the listener keeps asking questions about Linda and her mother. It is still possible to be curious about people if we dislike them. If the listener has unanswered questions, they will keep listening. Feeling for the characters won't come if there's no story.

The play could be about Mother's sudden addiction to online gambling and eventual bankruptcy. The listener may only want find out why Mother has gone down this route and see if she survives. We listen to know what happens next, not because we think, 'Oh she seems a sympathetic character.'

STORY TIME

To make a strong start to a radio drama, we need to return again and again to our first memory of storytelling, of being a child listening to someone tell a tale. 'Once upon a time there was a talking table... Once upon a time there was a little boy called James who lived under the sea... Once upon a time there was a yellow bear...' Children's story openings throw in a word or concept right away that promises the unusual or exciting. 'Once upon a time there was a table' isn't going to do it. We need a table that can dance, a table made entirely from cheese or a table that's waiting for someone called Godot. So check – are the first moments of your drama promising magic tables or are you just telling the listener about the furniture?

The magic table may be a great character, full of wisecracks and wisdom, but what is it doing? Is it on a quest? Is it in conflict with irritating table parents? Is it fighting to the death with an evil woodworm? How the table is as a character will quickly lose our interest if it isn't doing something with all that eloquence and charm.

A MAN WALKS INTO A ROOM

In film, a man walks into a room and takes the phone off the hook. We ask ourselves why he does this and who he is. The first moment of a radio play should be like this. Who is that? What are they doing and why?

We have to tease the audience. If the speaker says, 'Mother, you're late, I suppose you've been online gambling again,' then we've had too many questions answered. Unless Mother's comeback is, 'No, it's not that, something awful has happened.'

Then we're interested again. The online gambling isn't the answer to the question. We need to know what the awful thing is. Although we also now know that Mother has her character flaw and may be more interesting than a mother who's late because she's been too absorbed in her knitting again.

Asking questions and providing clues is the way to keep a listener listening. Give the answers too early, or too late and they may wander off. They may feel there's nothing to find out or they may feel confused. Many viewers gave up on the TV series *Lost* because they were fed up with endless new mysteries and no answers. If *Lost* were a radio series, they'd have been even more impatient because they didn't have all those attractive semi-clad people on a beach to look at.

WRITING LINE BY LINE

If you feel panic-stricken about getting your story across using only words and sound, you may begin to overwrite. Remember, if you get to the end and feel the audience needs more information, you can go back and thread in those extra clues. More producers complain about writers new to radio overwriting than writers being too sparse with their information.

The trick is to think more about holding the listener's interest than getting the information across. Perhaps, as with Becket or Pinter, the writer never tells us the whole story. Yet from moment to moment, we want to know what happens next, and will the next moment reveal a little more?

For practice, try writing a string of opening moments. How much information can you get across in the first three lines, while still posing questions to keep the listener interested? The amount of information you inadvertently drop in might surprise you. In a line we can glean a character's age, sex, mood, country of origin. We can glean their intention in the scene. Do they come into a room and ask, 'Is anybody there?' or say 'I know you're there!'?

Perhaps they say something more bizarre to attract the listener's attention: 'OK, everyone, I've checked and it is all cherry ice cream falling outside, not snow.' The line is establishing another world as well as getting us to ask who this man is and what he wants everyone to do about the cherry ice cream.

Sometimes writing an opening moment for practice can lead you into a story. You've reminded yourself of something; asked yourself a question you'd now like to have answered. Line by line you could build a play that you found hiding in that tiny moment. Every good radio play starts with a good tiny moment.

Beginning with your small moment, the start of the first scene, experiment with ways to make it ask more questions, rather than give us information that we won't need to know until the end of the play. For example, a character says, 'I've come to the sea. I hate the sea.' Plenty of questions there: who is 'I' and why come to a place they hate? Who are they talking to?

Perhaps they're in their car, talking on the phone. The other person might say, 'It was his idea I suppose.' More questions: who is 'he' and who is on the phone?

Keep building this until you feel a saturation point has been reached and it's time for a few answers before you move on to the next set of questions. There's no way of knowing when you've reached this point except with practice and instinct – rather like knowing the pulling point of a car when you're learning to drive. You just learn to feel it.

START FAR AWAY

If you really want to write a story about a failed love affair but are worried that there are already a lot of stories like that, begin with something far away from the story. Begin with a happy, newly married character arguing with a lonely, busybody neighbour. (The neighbour will be their only friend at the end.) Begin with a character discovering Umayyad treasure in the Jordanian desert. (It will be the obsession with Umayyads, or the newly found wealth that destroys their love life.)

If you know how your story ends, make sure the beginning doesn't give this away. Or if you have a story where most people know the ending – Oscar Wilde's marriage goes very wrong for instance – start with the least well-known character or an invented character. Start with the wife, or an invented character imagining that the marriage is going well. The intrigue could be to see how they get to the knowledge that the audience already has – that this is not going to end happily. The surprise could be that they knew all along that the marriage was doomed, but decided to pretend otherwise. If the end of the story is already well-known, begin somewhere that makes it a challenge for you to reach the facts of the ending. This will intrigue the listener – how will the couple get from here to disaster?

Another story could have a known happy ending, so start amid disaster.

Let the audience know as soon as possible that although they may have the answers, you still have questions they haven't thought of. They may know where the journey ends, but they don't know the route you've chosen to take them there. If your story is about Oscar Wilde, for example, have a man we don't know come into the room first of all. We will want to know who this man is and what he has to do with Oscar Wilde. If you begin with Oscar Wilde, have him come into a room for reasons we wouldn't expect.

CREATING FROM THE UNKNOWN

When you only have words to work with, it is worth making notes of how little the listener needs to know to make the story effective. A man walks into a room: what is he doing? Is someone else in the room? We may not need to know anything about the man who has walked into the room except that he is hiding something and imagines that he's alone. Perhaps what he's hiding is a murder weapon. How can we show this on radio? Do we hear his inner thoughts? Perhaps there is someone else in the room who asks him, 'Was that a knife?'

Does he confide in the person or does he get cornered into giving an answer before he kills them too? Is this a monologue so that we hear his fears of being caught? Who has he killed in the first instance and why? Is the second person an accomplice who'd told him to use a gun not a knife? How much do we need to know about this second character? How do we convey the information? For the start we only need to attract attention, create curiosity and build tension.

For practice, try writing a version of this story outline rather than the story you have had burning in your brain for years. This way you can stick to the mechanics rather than confusing yourself with all the things you've imagined about your own characters and story. Build something from nothing to learn how to build. Then try out the skills you've learnt to build your own 'dream house'.

For the time being, try building this as a dialogue without the convenience of inner thoughts to explain any of the actions. So, a man walks into a room and hides something... Perhaps it's something more bizarre than a murder weapon. Who else is in the room? Are they supposed to be there? Perhaps they are in league against someone outside the room. How do they speak? What do they say?

DON'T LISTEN TO THE MUSIC

Part of the opening of a play will be sound. It could be music, which is often useful to establish a timeframe, but not necessarily – after all, people listen to 1950s music today. It could be scary music to show we're in a horror genre, but really, unless it's a high-octane spoof, that might be a little corny. It could be happy music to establish a mood, but it always more interesting to have music that runs counter to the mood.

While you're starting to write radio drama, and possibly long after, it might a useful exercise to ban yourself from the use of music. Think about other sounds and how to use them to establish time, place and mood. Make a list of the different sounds you can think of. If necessary, invest in a sound effects CD. Close your eyes and listen to this as a way to kick-start yourself into thinking about all the sounds there are in the world other than music. Listen and consider how evocative the most commonplace sounds can be – birdsong, a match being struck, computer keys tapping, pages turning. Think of obviously dramatic sounds – a helicopter, a scream, a slammed door – and then try to make them the start of a scene where our expectations are thwarted; that is, the scene that follows is calm, romantic, comical or reassuring.

Use sound to counterpoint or undercut what's going on. For example, there's screaming in the background but the characters are nurses in an emergency ward, used to zoning out the distressing sound and going about their other business, gossiping about a fun night out they've just had. The listener can't zone it out, however, so the happy chatty scene has a constant tension – a threat that the contentment is bound to be short-lived.

Alternatively, you can begin with two characters having a screaming row while in the background there is happy laughter. Or our characters are in an attack helicopter but talking about what they like to wear on the beach. Will we find out who is laughing? Will our characters ever make it to the beach? Questions don't have to be asked directly. The sound can suggest questions because it quickly contradicts or undermines the dialogue.

> A radio moment that really stands out in my memory is the last thirty seconds of a *Journey Into Space* episode I heard when I must have been seven or eight, in the 1950s. They're the first landing on the moon – dead world – then somebody or something knocks on the outside of the space ship. Perfect!
>
> Mike Walker, radio dramatist

WHAT'S THAT NOISE?

Let's imagine some simple openings with a sound and a person interacting. We will get to questions and storytelling very quickly.

We hear a dog barking. What is it barking at? A man comes out of a door and curses the dog. Who is he? What is his relationship with the dog?

We hear a dog howling? Why is it howling? A child comes running along the street and asks the dog what's wrong. Who is the child? What is his relationship with the dog?

We hear a dog barking. What is it barking at? A woman greets the dog warily. Why is the woman so worried by the dog? Is she up to no good? Is the dog dangerous? Is she simply scared of dogs?

The noise that a dog makes might signify different things. Perhaps the character's reaction can run counter to the type of noise the dog makes. The dog is frenzied but the person is calm. Or the dog is joyful but the person is unnerved. Why?

Similarly a simple knock on a door can lead in many directions. What kind of door is it? Is it internal or external, heavy or flimsy? What kind of knock is it? Is it timid, angry or matter-of-fact? Who is knocking? Who answers the door? Perhaps no one answers the door and that is the start of the story.

If your story is about a man who has gone missing, the knocking without answer could be a strong beginning. It could provoke a neighbour to tell the caller that they haven't seen the man for days. The person knocking could explain themselves or be evasive. The neighbour could be indifferent or concerned, or could tell the caller that a string of people have been looking for the man. Say the neighbour's answer is the latter. The caller, let's call her Linda again, could ask what sort of people these were. Perhaps the neighbour tells her they were all young women, much younger than the man. The neighbour might comment that she thinks this is a bit rum. Linda, however, doesn't and haughtily tells the neighbour that her missing father tutored A-level mathematics. The neighbour then suggests that he's on holiday. Linda tells her this is impossible, as her father telephoned her an hour ago telling her to come round urgently.

This could be when Linda's mother with the online gambling problem turns up and says she's late because an awful thing has happened. The police have phoned her say her husband had just been run over. They're no longer needed at the house but at the hospital intensive care unit. Perhaps now we need to ask a new sort of question? Who is Linda anyway? Has she got other things going on in her life besides the antics and tragedies of her parents? Perhaps she can't believe she now has to go to the hospital because she's supposed to be at the airport saying goodbye to her lover. Perhaps she goes to the airport, her father dies and the lover dumps her. It could turn out that the father urgently wanted to see her because he discovered the lover was the father of one of his teenage pupils. Meanwhile Mother....

WHOSE STORY IS IT ANYWAY?

At some point in writing this story you will have decided that it is Linda's story. If it is supposed to be the mother's story, then why are with her the least? Why isn't it her decision to choose between going to the airport and the hospital? As a very general rule, the first person we meet, who does the most, who has the most things happen to them in the early scenes, is the person whose point-of-view we follow. However, the story does not have to be about them. It may be the father's story that is unravelled, or the mother's that Linda has to keep track of. Linda may have her own dilemmas with lovers at the airport, but her overriding preoccupation is with her mother's situation. Perhaps she discovers that mother's debts have led to the father being run over deliberately by loan sharks. We follow Linda and take clues from her as to what is the most important thing in the story.

So the important information we need in the first scenes is who are we following. As we've established, it doesn't matter if they are a liar or confused or mistaken. It doesn't matter if it isn't their story. Returning to a central character gives the story a clear shape. However, we don't have to be with Linda all the time. We can go to a conversation between the father and mother. This conversation could tell us something about Linda and her situation that Linda doesn't know. So that when we see Linda racing to weep over her lover, we know she's made a mistake – her father's told her mother that the lover is a no-good liar.

A story can also have more than one point-of-view character. Perhaps Linda and her mother have different takes on the same story. We follow Linda and her heartbreak. We also follow mother and her gambling problems, but for both of them the overriding preoccupation is the dying father. If the mother knows that his being run over is her fault, she may be trying to hide this from Linda. Perhaps Linda comes to understand that her father wasn't great and drove mother to gamble. The two point-of-view characters are approaching the same story in different ways and for different reasons, and may react to the end of it in different ways.

Two characters leading us through the same story have to be returned to the core story all the time. They may have their sub-plots and other preoccupations, but these have to keep relating to the heart of the story they share, because it could be the only thing they share. If we are finding out about a murder victim from the point-of-view of a detective and the murderer, the topic of the victim has to recur in their separate stories, otherwise what are they doing in the same play?

KEEP IN SHAPE

If you start your story and it gets messy after about six scenes, go back to the start. Are you introducing the right person or persons first? Are you following the character or characters whose take on events will be the most interesting? Has it confused matters to have more than one point-of-view? Is the story too thin if there is only one point-of-view?

The story can be about the point-of-view character or not. What needs to be clear from the start is that the point-of-view character has a main thing that they need to find out. What they find out can be about themselves, or it can be about someone else. They can find out that the murder victim was their lost brother and so finding out the truth of the case has involved them profoundly. They can find out that the murder victim ran a home for starving orphans and although nothing to do with the point-of-view character, what they find out makes the victim's story more distressing.

Think about the classic film *The Third Man*. Scene after scene goes by until we catch a glimpse of Harry Lime. Other characters talk about him all the time and the story is about him. Yet it is not him who we follow. We follow the people who will tell us about him. We're only interested in the characters we follow for what they can uncover about Harry Lime. In *The Third Man*, the other characters have stories, but Harry Lime is the main story, the main thing that everyone needs to ask questions about. The other characters have to return to discussing him and looking for him, or the shape of the story is lost. Once he is dead, the other characters stories are not so interesting because they were only part of the mechanics to help us follow Harry Lime's story.

Decide who is telling the story and who the story is about. The variations on this don't matter as much as sticking to the rules you establish. If you start with one character and they disappear half way into the story, who are we following? Who is our proxy detective?

If you begin following two, three or half a dozen characters, having decided on multiple points-of-view, be sure that they each contribute something to the story that the others can't. Be sure that they all stick to asking questions and finding answers to the same story. Otherwise you could end up with not one play but six.

UNRELIABLE WITNESSES

In some stories, a person is their own detective. For example, they might want to find out how they lost their fortune and ended up bewildered in the gutter. In this case it is easy for the listener to see who to follow through the story. Except the clues we find may destroy the sympathy we have for the character in the beginning. Perhaps they deserve their bad fortune.

If someone is poor, bedridden or victimized, we assume they are asking the right questions. Why me? How did I deserve this? Perhaps clues will be dropped to make the listener distrust the central character eventually, and ask questions of their own.

There is an instinct that we probably brought with us from childhood – that we trust the narrator of a story. It might be interesting to consider telling your story from the point-of-view of someone who is telling lies about what happened. Eventually they may be confronted and crumble. For example, we may believe a character when she tells us that she won the lottery and now can't stop spending. She tells us a lot about the horrors of poverty she's lived with and how happy she is now. We enjoy the fun she's having. Later it might turn out she's embezzled from her company, which is about to go bankrupt, putting all her friends out of work, and she couldn't care less. She's tricked us with her charming storytelling.

Perhaps we can drop hints to the listener that this narrator or central character is a liar. We hear them lie to another character or they say something that makes us suspicious. This type of uncertainty is a good way to keep the listener interested.

If a storyteller says, 'I landed on the moon long before the crew of Apollo 11,' we immediately prick up our ears. How can that be true? Why are they saying that? Or we may hear a character tell someone that they've never learnt to drive, then in the next scene they're driving a taxi. We want to know why this person is lying. A lie at the opening of a play is like throwing a stone into a pond. Immediately you've created a splash.

EXAMPLE OF AN OPENING

To give an idea of how a radio play begins and continues here is a section from a simple forty-five-minute drama, *Poisoned by a Tree*. This is mostly a two-hander set in one room, so my tools for building the detective story were limited, but this can be helpful to a writer as the options aren't overwhelming. There aren't half a dozen characters to work into the scenes. There are few decisions to be made about how to move from place to place. The characters that appear can be developed at some leisure.

The story is really about Sarah and her relationship with her absent daughter. It is Barbara who drives the story because she wants to find out about

Sarah and the daughter. Barbara learns that there are questions to ask and wants answers. She is the proxy detective for the listener. Once Barbara indicates that there are questions to ask, the listener should then start asking their own questions.

In the next chapter, we'll look in more detail about devices used to build this play.

INT. HOSPITAL WARD 15.30 DAY 1

A SMALL HOSPITAL WARD – SIX BEDS. EMPTY EXCEPT FOR SARAH.

WARD DOOR BANGS OPEN.

BARBARA RUNS CLATTERING AND SKIDDING ACROSS THE WARD TO WINDOW.

1 **BARBARA**	Did you see that? Did you see it? It was one of those...things.
2 **SARAH**	Things? If any things had been in this ward I'd have noticed. It's as dull as a ditch and not a thing within yards.
3 **BARBARA**	It's gone. I thought it came over this way. I love them. Like sort of elephants aren't they? Flying elephants.
4 **SARAH**	Dull and I have a nurse that sees flying elephants. Good. Was it pink?
5 **BARBARA**	You're wicked you are, you just want me to look mad, but you did see it.
6 **SARAH**	It was an airship. They don't look like elephants. Barrage balloons look like elephants. Airships look like... Rugby balls.
7 **BARBARA**	It came right close to the front of the building, I thought they'd gone out of control, thought it was going to crash into us.
8 **SARAH**	They came over this side of the building in a perfectly orderly fashion and seemed to know exactly what they were doing.
9 **BARBARA**	What are they doing?
10 **SARAH**	It's an advertising thing isn't it? My daughter's company has one that flies around Peterborough with their name on. What I always wonder is, where are the people? The passengers and the crew and what have you.
11 **BARBARA**	In the bit underneath.
12 **SARAH**	Seems very small though. I'm sure I remember a film about a big famous airship that crashed or exploded and blew up or something and

there were loads of people inside, like on the QE2, dancing tea dances and that carry on. Or is this something else I'm thinking of?

13 **BARBARA**   Funny, we can go to Mars and the moon and we still run around overexcited about a bag of hot air in the sky.

14 **SARAH**   I know. I've lived in London half my life and would still stare up at an aeroplane.

15 **BARBARA**   No, I don't think an aeroplane's the same (**COMES OVER TO SARAH**) I better do your blood pressure and stuff.

16 **SARAH**   And stuff. It's the stuff I'd be worried about. (**BEAT**) There wasn't a phone call for me or anything?

17 **BARBARA**   You just had a load of visitors.

18 **SARAH**   You would bring the phone through, if there was a call, wouldn't you?

19 **BARBARA**   No, because I'm one of those evil type of nurses they make documentaries about.

20 **SARAH**   I saw a documentary about people who like to pretend to be doctors and nurses. A very common form of lunacy.

21 **BARBARA**   Oh, you caught me out. (**BEAT**) (**MOVES OFF**) I'll see you in a minute, I'll just go and get all the equipment I need for my life as a fake nurse. And don't worry, you always get your phone calls, because I like to listen in.

22 **SARAH**   You'd have a long listen for anything exciting in my phone calls. Anyway, why would someone phone if they were on their way?

23 **BARBARA**   There's no prize for the patient with the most visitors you know. Look at this place – Kew gardens.

24 **SARAH**   I find all these flowers round me very depressing. Funereal.

25 **BARBARA**   Stop that. Oh there it is. Look.

26 **SARAH**   Be nice to go up in an airship or something wouldn't it? If I was one of those rich fellas I'd fly about everywhere in airships... or balloons.

27 **BARBARA**   I'd get a stretch limo and a chauffeur.

28 **SARAH**   Not very imaginative.

29 **BARBARA**   I'm not. (**BEAT**) My brother had imagination. He went to Australia to do something about it and a poisonous tree burnt his arm.

30 **SARAH**   Liar.

31	**BARBARA**	No, it's a thing they've got out there in the rain forest.
32	**SARAH**	I suppose they'd have all kinds of things out there you wouldn't want to know about. Was he alright?
33	**BARBARA**	Well he's got a scar. Drives a cab in Lewisham now. The tree business, that was sort of the end of having imagination for him. Don't keep me talking here, according to something I saw on telly, I've got a 'spirit crushing timetable'. So there. (**MOVING AWAY**) I'll be back in a minute with the torture implements, and take it all out on you.
34	**SARAH**	(**TUTS**) Leave me alone with this foliage. It'll all rise up growing tendrils and choke me.

SOUND OF DISTANT PHONE RINGING

35	**BARBARA**	(**GOING**) Or poison you.
36	**SARAH**	There's that as well. Listen, get on with you, I can hear the phone ringing.
37	**BARBARA**	I'm going. Rush rush, see – the spirit crushing dog's life of a nurse.

SHE BANGS OUT OF WARD DOORS

DISTANT PHONE RINGS A MOMENT THEN CUTS

SARAH SIGHS. THEN 'TUTS'

(Excerpt from opening scenes of *Poisoned by a Tree by* Annie Caulfield.)

3 BUILDING THE STORY

ONCE WE'VE STARTED

We set up quesions, we provide limited information and some new questions. The play is beginning. Meanwhile the listener is deciding whether to go to the shops, or tackle the pile of ironing. They wouldn't mind doing the ironing if there were a play on the radio that held their attention.

Even if the writer starts a play well, they can't be sure of the listener's devotion. They've started listening, but will they stay? Will they stay but stop *actively* listening, drift off into their own daydreams about the day they can afford to pay someone else to do the ironing. Even if a person hasn't switched the radio off, they may not be listening.

As well as asking questions to keep the listener interested, there are other ways to hold their attention. One of these is to change the focus of a scene. Two people are chatting about one thing, then a new topic is mentioned. The new topic is clearly important, something we want to know about. We may return to the original topic but we are now impatient to know about the second topic.

Focus can be changed by altering the pace as well as the topic. A scene may start fast and agitated, then slow down, then become brisk again. In *Poisoned by a Tree*, there are few scene changes because the main character, Sarah, is bedridden. Changes of pace and conversational direction are essential to keep the story alive. There's a fast pace as Barbara comes in. The topic is the airship, but in speech sixteen, just as things are slowing down, Sarah asks about a telephone call. This is a new topic and asks bigger questions – why is the call important and who is it from? Sarah isn't lonely, and we hear about her many visitors, so who is this person that counts more than everyone else? The question of the phone returns, with even more anxiety attached to it. By the time we hear the phone ringing in the distance, it's not just a sound effect, it's a new character. It could be providing answers. It also creates new tension. Will Barbara get there in time? Will the call be for Sarah?

OUTSIDE THE ROOM

Another problem with the opening scene of *Poisoned by a Tree* is that there are only two characters and it is one very long scene. Every few lines a new element has to be introduced to keep it lively. Mentioning outside characters adds another dimension. Sarah has a daughter, Barbara has a brother; we have questions about them.

Go through a scene of yours, ideally a long one, and make sure that it is asking as many questions as possible. Some of these may never be answered. Perhaps Barbara's brother is fairly irrelevant, but we need him to make a point about how people become disillusioned. Yet at this point in the story he's someone to speculate about. Will he turn up? Will he crash his taxi and end up in the hospital providing essential transplant parts for Sarah? Once a character is mentioned they have potential. They may be someone the listener needs to know more about. Or not. At this point the listener doesn't know, they just notice there's a new piece of information.

VOICES OFF

Sometimes it is interesting to hear people outside the room of a scene. For example, if a scene is in a prison cell, the prisoners may hear yells from other prisoners that create anxiety. A lonely character may hear happy laughing neighbours. Happy laughing characters may hear a sobbing neighbour. This may only lead to a subplot or an occasional distraction, but it helps build a world around the scene. Especially when you have a limited number of characters with which to create your story.

A person who doesn't appear directly might be making a racket outside. The lead character might then have to go outside and remonstrate with them. This gives the second character a chance to nose around the living room; perhaps they find something in a drawer they're going to have to ask about.

Perhaps a laughing happy family next door makes a lonely central character look at his life. He might decide to go out speed dating, and finds bliss or complications – and all thanks to the family we never meet. A character who doesn't appear can do many jobs for the writer.

As an exercise, try writing a few opening scenes and introducing characters who will never appear, although we can hear them. The main characters can discuss what they're up to. What will these characters contribute to the main story? What will be the end of the subplot of this person? How will you resolve this without giving them a speaking part?

TENSION

Look for other tensions in the scene. In *Poisoned by a Tree*, Barbara has a job to do. We wonder when she'll get back to it. We also wonder what's wrong with Sarah. How serious is it? It can be useful to give characters something that they should be doing other than being in the scene. It means the listener is aware that the scene can't go on indefinitely. It can give the dialogue an urgency. Think about how many hospital scenes happen in the operating theatre or emergency room – characters can't chat too much when they have someone's innards in their hands. And something could start beeping signifying disaster at any moment.

Imagine a place where people could be talking but have somewhere else to be. A station platform or a bus stop are good standbys. Will they miss the train or will they forget to flag down the bus? Will they get the answers to the questions that they want before they have to leave?

Imagine other places where characters will need to leave at any moment, such as people at a supermarket checkout, or in an office with a telephone ringing in the background; or a postman on his rounds. Flesh out the characters' lives outside the dialogue and create a sense that they will need to leave the conversation soon.

ANXIETY

- If two mothers are talking at an adventure playground, are their children about to come over and demand attention, or fall off the pirate castle and demand panicked action?
- If at the top of a scene, a character says that they have a money problem, this might simply indicate why they are anxious in the scene or alternatively might mean that bailiffs are about to rush in the door.
- A person is trying to find a lost child. They have a limited number of units remaining on their mobile. They have to make a succession of succinct, panicked calls to people they don't know well.
- Two women are robbing a bank. One makes a chance remark that tells the other she has slept with her husband. They have to bicker, and still hurry up and rob the bank.

Consider giving your characters a problem in the scene, then add an additional one, such as illness or financial worry or sudden horrific revelation. The problems added in may not turn into anything of substance in the play, but they tell us more about the characters, create excitement and add a little more for the listener to speculate about.

Creating tension and anxiety within each scene as you go along is the way to keep an audience with you. You may be working towards a great pay-off, an astounding twist in the tale at the end of your play – but many people will have wandered away in the meantime. Radio drama is about what is happening now.

CHANGING FOCUS

Usually in a radio play a scene would run a quarter of the length of this opening scene from *Poisoned by a Tree*, maybe less. We'd move somewhere else. Changing scenes can help keep the interest. Changing from two people talking to a crowd scene, or from two people talking to a monologue, is a way of keeping interest by refocusing the audience's attention. Were we to go from this pleasant hospital scene to a scene where three people argue ferociously, screaming at each other, our attention would have been pulled up, refocused. However, if we return, as this play does, to the same two characters talking, we need to change something. In this play Sarah's anxiety about the telephone increases, and Barbara has to cheer her up even more. Their relationship shifts in tone, refocusing the listener's attention. This is not the light-hearted play that the audience was listening to in the beginning; there is a building tragedy. Starting a sad play in a light-hearted mood wrong-foots the audience. This keeps their attention. They think they are comfortable in the notion of what they're listening to, but then they are disturbed.

With a play that is predominantly a two-hander, your work of holding interest is in the constant shifts of topic, in the changes of pace and in the scattering of new questions as the earlier ones are answered. If the characters are looking at something in particular, or doing something, you need to suddenly change this. For example, two people may be talking in a prison cell, while having lunch. One suddenly realizes that he has been given a metal spoon – can he use it to tunnel out? No. The walls are too hard, there's no hope. They return to the lunch and their earlier conversation, but the mood has been changed, and the listener's attention drawn in a new direction.

CHARACTERS ON THE MOVE

If your play moves from location to location, try to provide contrasts. Moving from a hospital scene to an office is to go from a quiet place to another quiet place. Why not move to a street? If moving from quiet place to quiet place, perhaps the characters can be followed as they move. If two nurses are going from a hospital ward to their office, their walk to get there will not only tell us they've moved – it will give us a brisker tone. The way people talk when they walk is not the same as when they are sitting around.

As you build the play, keep asking yourself what the characters are doing and where are they? Is there a reason why they can't move? If not, move them. Even if they only leave the office to walk down the corridor to the canteen – they're active, and new things are happening.

> How do people know where they are? I think in some ways it's more important for people to know where they aren't! In other words, they need to know that the scene they're listening to now, is not the scene we've just heard. Some scene settings – inside a church for instance – can be realized almost instantaneously, with an echo plate and a touch of organ. But if you're moving from someone's lounge to someone's bedroom, the acoustic difference might be very subtle indeed – in which case the new location needs to be registered through what characters say, and how they behave. My advice to new radio playwrights would be, wherever possible, to vary locations from scene to scene. The radio audience, listening on less than perfect equipment, only really distinguishes between three different acoustics – 'live' (e.g. inside a room), 'dead' (e.g. a field) and 'live with echo' (e.g. a church, a bathroom). It's useful for writers to bear this in mind when devising scenes.
>
> Gordon House, former head of BBC World Service Drama.

CONTINUING THE PLAY

Throughout a radio play, it is predominantly dialogue that will tell the story. All the questions you want the listener to ask and clues you need to drop in have to be put in to credible words. So let's assume you have started the play, you know what the story is and who we follow. You have an arresting opening sound effect and an intriguing opening conversation. What next? People talking for forty-five minutes? Maybe interspersed with some car doors, dogs barking and phones ringing? How can that work? The answer really is still line by line.

4 DIALOGUE

We all know bad dialogue when we hear it and producers all have their favourite examples.

> Perhaps the foremost challenge for playwrights for radio is correct judgement of the economy of statement. New writers can tend either to fail to create enough information for the ear or become over-explicit. This is what gives rise to classic radio over-writing:
>
> *WILSON: You may be a fourteen stone athlete with a crossbow, Johnson, but it's no good trying to get past me. I'm standing between you and the doorway and holding a sharpened broom-handle.*
>
> Here Wilson is made to describe a situation which in reality would not require description and for which, given Johnson's size and fitness, Wilson wouldn't have time to say anyway before a crossbow bolt impaled him to the doorpost.
>
> John Taylor, Creative Director, Fiction Factory Productions

Producers I interviewed all mentioned the inexperienced writer's panicked tendency towards over-writing. Words matter so much in radio that we need to use them sparingly. One producer suggests going through a scene, just as an exercise, and ruthlessly cutting the dialogue in half. Does it still make sense? Often it does. You may lack a little colour and humour that needs to be added back in, but the exercise is useful to show how very little needs to be said to tell a story.

Writers feel they need to describe things for the listener, usually far too much. They have characters say things like 'I haven't seen you in that blue dress before.' Why do we need to know the dress is blue? If there's a reason beyond a worry that the listener won't be able to imagine the dress, take out the adjective. People will see their own version of the dress.

> Mistakes? There's the 'this gun in my left hand is loaded' type of mistake of course, but normally people overwrite as they feel the need to compensate for the lack of visuals.
>
> Sally Avens, BBC comedy producer

Adjectives are the words that can be lost the most in radio dialogue. If they're purely to paint a picture, they may be a distraction rather than an enhancement. Where words are few, the fact that a dress is blue, yellow or pink is deemed by the listener to have some significance, simply because it's been mentioned.

If a character says, 'I've never seen you in a tight dress before,' this could be more important. Why is the woman (presumably it's a woman) suddenly wanting to show off her curves? Is the type of dress important to character and plot development? Why are we mentioning it at all? Is it to indicate that a character is up to something, is changing their habits, or has had all their baggage full of trousers stolen? If there's no reason, there's no room in a radio play for small talk. Forget trying to write in a wardrobe department, move on with the story.

> A radio play is more like a charcoal sketch than an oil painting. It's enough to see the shape of the story.
>
> Jeremy Mortimer, senior BBC drama producer

TAKE OUT WORDS

Other words to take out are those directions to the actors in brackets before a speech. This can mean holding your nerve a little. If you really want an actor to sound angry, you panic and put (ANGRY) ahead of the line. So often I've done this and realized in recording that anger is the wrong emotion. Perhaps the actor has taken the character in a different direction and decided the line should be non-committal or shocked. They'll either ask to ignore the direction, or do what you say without confidence.

Let the actors surprise you. Let them find their own way through a scene and a character. One of the reasons why it's essential to go to play recordings is to learn how often you've actually hamstrung an actor with your directions, rather than helping them. Your presence also means that if an actor is playing a line in a non-committal way, you can suggest to the director that they play it angrily. But having a little faith in the actors usually yields pleasant surprises when they read something into a character or a line that you didn't realize was there. Perhaps unconsciously you've made a character more sympathetic than you thought. Perhaps they're coming across as even angrier than you'd imagine, but because of the way the actor has built up to the moment, it works. Hold your nerve and see what the actors come up with.

An experienced actor told me they have learnt to ignore anything in brackets unless it says (WITH WHOLE COD IN MOUTH). It's useful for actors to know things like this, but not to have emotional performance dictated to them. If you really want the actor to sound angry, paint them into a corner. If the scene and their line have no possible tone other than anger, then you'll get what you want.

The reason for an emotion to be applied to a line should be in the line itself, or the preceding lines. Or even the following line. If a character says, 'There's no need to get angry,' it's pretty obvious to the actor playing the preceding line how they have to sound.

What do the Characters Know?

The characters in the play usually know where they are, what they're doing and what they're wearing. If you have a character say, 'We have to stay at this village fete until it ends,' then why doesn't the person with them know they're at a village fete? Aren't there sound effects and action to tell the audience we're at a garden fete?

If the character says, 'We have to stay at this wretched fete until the end,' then that is different. It is an emotion the speaker has about the fete that the other character may not know.

What about conveying information where the sound effects aren't there to help? An example could be a simple office setting; computer keyboards tend to be much quieter than typewriters so there's a location-creating effect lost to the modern writer. If a character comes in and says, 'You've got a very big office,' the person with the office knows this already, so why tell them? Unless the character who has come in is a decorator making an estimate. So talking about the size would be done with a sigh and followed by mention of an exorbitant projected fee.

The facts about the office can be incorporated into a line that does more. 'Your office is twice the size of mine,' gives emotion to the whole big office issue. Is this envy, praise or shock?

When you've written a scene, look at the dialogue for moments where the characters are telling each other things that they would already know. To return to the blue dress line, if a character says, 'I haven't seen you in that blue dress before,' the person in the dress already knows it is blue. The adjective needs to be there for another reason. Perhaps the character always wears the same black dress, so the comment would need to be followed by, 'I thought you only had the black one.' The change in dress colour needs to mean something or this is just wasted dialogue.

Information Communication

If you need to get a piece of information across, some simple tweaking of lines can communicate the information in ways in which people really do speak. Simple tweaking - and trimming.

For example: 'Don't talk to her like that, she's my mother.' Doesn't the other person know it's the speaker's mother? If they don't already know, this is an odd way to impart information in a stressful situation. Wouldn't it sound more natural as 'Don't talk to my mother like that.'

Or if someone says, 'Don't talk to her like that! Can't you see she's only a kid? You're frightening her.' The frightening person knows they're looking at a kid. The speaker has something urgent to say but is taking ages to say it. Perhaps this speech could pare right down to 'You're frightening the kid.'

Perhaps you want to start a play about people locked in a zoo for the night. Remember that they know they're in a zoo. So, 'I can't believe it, we're locked in the zoo! Do you think we'll be here all night?' is all a bit superfluous and melodramatic. Maybe they'd be more likely to say, 'We're locked in? We can't be, there must be some night zoo-keepers or something to let us out.'

Also, if you want characters to explain the situation they're in, have them trying to get out of it. People seldom stand around making speeches about what's happening to them, but they might vocalize solutions to their problems. Think of bizarre situations characters could be in at the start of a play. Look for ways to communicate what their problem is, without them describing it to the other characters who are in the same situation. Try to give them an active, argumentative or solution-finding line. This way the play starts with movement, conflicting emotions and characters about to do something – rather than describing their situation to each other.

HOW PEOPLE SPEAK

A good exercise is to spend a morning eavesdropping in a bus, café or pub – wherever you're likely to overhear conversations. If possible, tape the conversations and then write them down absolutely as they occur. Or try to remember them accurately, without editing them down to the highlights.

The first thing you'll notice is that people don't speak in full sentences all the time and they interrupt each other. People hesitate and often the conversation lapses altogether. And of course, people don't always say what they mean or mean what they say. The way people really speak is so full of holes, *non sequiturs* and meanderings that it is not very coherent, let alone dramatic. The trick is to go through your pieces of eavesdropping and decide what the core of the dialogue is.

Perhaps Mr Brown is telling Mr Grey that he has been to see his daughter in hospital where she's just had twins, but first, Mr Brown and Mr Grey meet at the bus stop. They have to greet each other, perhaps talk about the weather, the bus service, then finally Mr Grey asks about the daughter. Perhaps Mr Grey doesn't know what to say about the twins and his sole reactions is, 'Twins, blimey.' So after a pause Mr Brown has to pick up the conversational baton and talk about his father being a twin. Perhaps Mr Grey isn't very interested in this either and says, 'Oh, I see.' So the conversation lapses again.

The core of the dialogue is probably the information about the twins. What else is going on? If our story is about Mr Grey and his secret loathing for Mr Brown and his endless chatter, then we will trim the dialogue one way. If it is about Mr Brown's frustrated attempts to befriend Mr Grey, we will trim it another way. But we will need to trim it because real people use a lot of unnecessary words.

Perhaps the story is about the twins growing up to be serial killers, so this scene is an ironically joyful announcement of their birth. Mr Grey isn't important, but perhaps Mr Brown is remembering how excited he was about these twins who've gone to the bad.

In every dialogue scene, we need to hold on to the story ideas. Who are we following? Who is the story about? Remembering this will help us cut to the core of the dialogue.

To create a real sounding dialogue from a real scene we need to give a sketch of how the people talk, not an exact representation. There should be some pauses, some interruptions and *non sequiturs* – but not all of them, or the play would never get anywhere. Nevertheless, really listening to how people speak can help avoid dialogue that sounds too 'written', too articulate, too smooth, too free of personality.

> I know people talk in cliché all the time – I've just written 'join the dots' but when you hear the start of a sentence and have already finished in your head before the character, then your attention has been taken away from the play you're listening to. In effect you are saying, 'yeah, yeah', or 'yadder, yadder', or 'blah, blah' in your head and mentally turning off. Trying to think about how a character would say it differently sometimes helps me think in a deeper way about the character.
>
> Sarah Daniels, dramatist

MAKING SPEECHES

Even the cleverest people seldom speak articulately. If Mr Brown wants to discuss the genetics of multiple births with fellow scientist Mr Grey at the bus stop, he will still hesitate and leave sentences unfinished. He won't sound as though he is reading from an essay on the subject. No matter how expert these two men are, the listener may not be a geneticist. A scientific word or two might drop into the conversation but overall, the conversation needs to be comprehensible to the average non-geneticist. It is a matter of stylization.

If Mr Brown has a theory he needs to make Mr Grey accept, it won't sound real if he gushes it out fully-formed as lecture at the bus stop. Mr Grey would interrupt, and Mr Brown would interrupt himself with a few, 'Do you see what I means?'. Very few people speak in long speeches without checking they are being understood and still have the attention of the listener.

Also, if Mr Grey is another expert, he may not need many things explaining to him. Perhaps Mr Brown is trying to explain the science of twins to his exhausted daughter who has just given birth to twins, so it will be in language the listener will understand.

Giving characters uneven levels of knowledge enables explanation to happen in a way that sounds likely.

WORDS IN THE RIGHT ORDER

If a character says, 'I'll draw the curtains,' then we hear the curtain sound, this is a waste of time. If, however, we hear the sound of the curtains being drawn just as the character says, 'I'll draw the curtains,' then there can be a tiny moment of intrigue where the listener thinks, 'What's that noise?' – a question half formed that is then answered.

Also, it is only worth drawing the curtains if someone in the play is about to take their clothes off, is on the run from the police or has a sudden phobia to sunlight. Anything that happens should happen for a reason, otherwise don't waste dialogue mentioning it.

TIMEWASTING

It's also important to remember the screen-writing adage that you should start in the middle of a scene. A scene can end in the middle of a line of dialogue; a new scene can start in the middle of another person's line of dialogue a hundred miles away. In radio you can cut as in a film, so there's no reason for people to have a fully resolved conversation. And there's certainly no reason for people to be coming in and out of rooms.

Here's an example of time wasting.

A KNOCK ON THE DOOR

MAN	Who is it?
VICAR	It's the vicar.
MAN	Ah come in, Vicar, it's open.

DOOR OPENS.

VICAR	Ah, Bill, sorry to disturb you, it's just something a bit awkward has happened.
MAN	A bit awkward?
VICAR	Yes, it's your son. I saw him in a pawn shop with that stolen church silver.

First of all, I'd say don't write plays about things like this because it's exa-ctly what people think they hate about radio plays – all middle England and people on free and easy terms with vicars. However, there's a lot more wrong with it. We're worn out before we get to the heart of the matter. In real life, the vicar might actually take a lot longer to get to the point if Bill is his friend. So we need to find dramatic ways to get there rather than an inaccurate depiction of real life circumlocution.

Also, the big moment is pre-empted. We're told something is a bit awkward and then it is more than awkward. This might work in a comedy where the vicar says something is a bit awkward and it turns out the son has dug up and eaten the contents of the graveyard. If we are looking for drama in this scene, it's more effective not to pre-empt any emotional response. The vicar could tell Bill, 'Something's happened.' And Bill will know to ask, 'Something bad, I take it?' because Bill can see the vicar's expression.

It might be better to go back to the start of the whole scene and consider it more carefully as a whole. Let's imagine it is the first scene in the play. By the time the vicar is in, half the listeners will have gone. What is this play going to be about? Let's say it's about Bill's gradual discovery that his son, his pride and joy, is a heroin addict and Bill's eventual inability to cope. Why can't he cope? Because he is a high-achieving perfectionist who thought he had the perfect son.

One of the faults with the basic scene we began with is that it tells us so little about the characters. They aren't really doing anything other than delivering their dialogue. We have no sense of what kind of people they are, except that one is a vicar.

We should always try to have more than one thing going on in a scene. Building in character details as well as plot is a way to bring things to life and make the speeches sound as though they come from real people. We can establish who Bill is by placing him somewhere other than his house. Perhaps he is in the drive, tinkering with the engine of his vintage sports car. Then the vicar can just walk right up to him, with no need for messing about with doors.

In order to convey awkwardness the vicar can say nothing. Let Bill find out what he wants. And if the vicar and Bill are friends, why would he refer to 'your son'? Wouldn't the vicar know the boy's name?

The engine tinkering gives Bill something to be doing other than sitting in his house waiting for vicars to chance by. It also gives them both something to distract them from the main point of the discussion. In order to get to the point of a dialogue, it's important for characters to have a distraction. Contradictory as this may seem, it gives the dialogue texture, while allowing for a naturalistic sounding hesitation and evasiveness. It gives the listener more to imagine if there's conversation about the engine of a Triumph Stag, rather than strung out hesitations and stallings such as:

VICAR   The thing is, Bill, I've something important to tell you.
BILL   Something important?
VICAR   Yes, not good news, I'm afraid.
BILL   Oh. What is it?
VICAR   The thing is, I was passing that pawn shop in the high street the other day...
BILL   The one by the bakery?
VICAR   That's the one. The thing is...

And so on, tediously, in an attempt to make the dialogue sound real. Far better in fact to have the vicar rush up to Bill and blurt out the facts:

VICAR   Bill, I've been looking for you all over. The person who stole the church silver, I've a horrible feeling it might be Jason.
BILL   My son doesn't steal.
VICAR   Bill, I'm sorry, I saw him in the high street pawn shop with it.

At least with this, the job is done. We've found an economical way to tell who Jason is and how Bill perceives his son. What we lack is any atmosphere or sense of character. Let's try it again, this time with the vintage car.

EXT. DRIVE.

BILL IS TINKERING WITH
THE ENGINE OF A TRIUMPH STAG.

VICAR	(**APPROACHING**) How many of these monstrosities do you need?
BILL	The Triumph Stag is an elegant machine, Vicar, a very elegant machine.
VICAR	One is elegant; four is an obsession.
BILL	This is number five, what would you call that?
VICAR	A lot of time under the bonnet.
BILL	The tinkering is the joy of it. Grab a spanner, join in, very good for the soul.
VICAR	I'm sure it is.
BILL	Besides, there's no one round here I'd trust with these beauties.
VICAR	No.

PAUSE

BILL	Are you looking for a donation?
VICAR	Worse than that. It's about the stolen church silver.
BILL	You're too trusting, you should lock the church door.
VICAR	I saw Jason in town trying to pawn it.
BILL	No, you didn't.
VICAR	I wouldn't tell you if I wasn't certain.
BILL	Why would my son need to steal?

It's still not perfect but we have more sense of who these people are. The awkwardness is established by the vicar's withdrawal from the banter, then his silence. We have a question for a moment. Who is Jason? Then the question is answered. We have a sense of being in a place, and we can visualize the scene. We know the characters are familiar with each other enough to tease each other. Another element is starting to emerge; the two men have different ways of talking. The vicar is wry and careful; Bill is ebullient, full of certainty. The way people are influences how they talk and vice versa.

CHARACTER IN DIALOGUE

One producer told me that if she can lay a ruler over the names of a play's characters on the left-hand side of the page and not be able to tell who is speaking, then the play isn't working. This has nothing to do with accent. Some writers put in apostrophes, phonetic renderings of words and dialect words to show what a person's accent sounds like, but this isn't the most important way that dialogue is differentiated.

People with different accents have different speech patterns. To write the difference between a Yorkshirewoman and a woman from Northern Ireland, the important thing to listen for is the rhythms and different word orderings. Sarah, back in the *Poisoned by a Tree* excerpt, for instance, is from Northern

43

Ireland. It's an accent I know well, so I can hear the way she'd order her words. Barbara is a Londoner, another way of speaking I'm used to hearing. If I were to write a Yorkshire character, I'd have to find someone to listen to in order to get the rhythm right, if not the Yorkshire words. Sometimes as a last resort, in a hurry, I might simply write in that a character has a Yorkshire accent in the directions and hope for a Yorkshire actor – invariably they'll put their head up in recording and say, 'I wouldn't use that word.' Or, 'in Yorkshire we'd say it this way round.'

I feel happier with what I've written if this doesn't happen. And it's always interesting how many subtle differences there are in the way the same language is spoken in different regions.

VOICES

What if the characters have similar accents? They will still speak differently. A character may be confident, timid, depressed, cynical, inarticulate, pompous or the oldest swinger in town. This will change the way they speak and the sort of words they use.

As an exercise, try taking all these dominant characteristics and writing dialogue to convey them. Try a confident person talking to a cynical person, an inarticulate person talking to a pompous person, and so on. Give them something meaty but impersonal to discuss – the death of a neighbour, for instance. Once the scene is written, give it to someone else to read and ask them what kind of person they think each character is. Have you given enough clues? Too many?

A character's emotional state will also change their speech. If someone is tired, stressed, happy, bitter, sad, angry, nervous and so on, this can come out in the pattern of the words they use, and the way they interact. Is it with energy? Are they monosyllabic or effusive? Are the punchy words expressing fury? Are the soft words expressing sadness?

Let's say that Linda is tired and her mother, Jane, is angry. Linda has found a repossession notice for the mother's house.

LINDA	I was going to make a cup of coffee.
JANE	Why didn't you ask me. This is my house.
LINDA	I was trying to save you the... Anyway, this was stuffed in a mug.
JANE	I don't go to your house and start opening cupboards.
LINDA	You wouldn't find repossession notices in my mugs.
JANE	I wouldn't find things because I wouldn't be snooping around looking for things.
LINDA	All I wanted was some coffee.
JANE	I can deal with my own problems. I don't need you snooping.
LINDA	Fine, Mum. I'll leave you to it then.

JANE	You're not going to help me?
LINDA	Maybe. I don't know. I need to go home.

Mother has energy; she changes direction and punches out her words. Linda winds down, retreats and keeps to the attitude she began with. Anger has energy. Tiredness retreats. We also sense that Jane may be manipulative and Linda may be sensible, verging on the self-righteous. Character as well as mood emerges.

What if the topic made their ways of talking less obvious? What if they were only talking about coffee?

LINDA	I've made the coffee.
JANE	I didn't want any.
LINDA	It's made now.
JANE	So you're staying all evening then?
LINDA	I can't, Mum.
JANE	I don't like that much milk.
LINDA	You didn't want coffee.
JANE	If I've got to drink it...
LINDA	Have mine, it's got less...
JANE	Why did you make coffee if you're not staying?
LINDA	To wake me up for the drive.
JANE	I don't make coffee in your house without asking.
LINDA	Don't you?
JANE	Of course I don't, I respect people's privacy.
LINDA	I needed coffee.

People can be talking about nothing much and tie each other in emotional knots. Eventually this conversation would have to go somewhere. Perhaps Linda finds a burst of energy and storms out in a rage. Perhaps her mother responds to Linda's tiredness with sympathy in the end. Or Mother's mood escalates and she screams at Linda to just leave.

As an exercise, try writing a basic scene like this with characters in different moods. Keep them talking about something apparently innocuous and see how you can change it with different moods and characteristics. What will also emerge as you try to make changes is a different kind of mother and daughter. In this version Linda is a bit of a martyr and emotionally weak as well as being tired, while mother is energetic and belligerent. How they talk to each other starts to tell a story about their relationship as well as their characters. In your basic scene, how many different relationships, characters and moods can you convey just in the way people speak?

WHAT ELSE ARE THEY TALKING ABOUT?

Linda and her mother, Jane, are in the kitchen bickering about coffee. Is this all that's going on in the scene? Perhaps Linda is exhausted because she's trying to sort out mother's finances and discovers it's all worse than she thought. Perhaps this is the scene that we need to build to the discovery of mother as a gambler, until the big crisis when the estranged father is run over by angry loan sharks.

With any dialogue scene, make sure that you know what the key piece of information you need to get across will be. Then build a dialogue about something else that gets the characters to that information logically, or to an emotional pitch where it will be blurted out. Try at the same time to have their characters emerge and have them doing something.

> Whenever people talk to me about the weather, I always feel certain that they mean something else.
>
> Gwendolen, in *The Importance of Being Earnest* by Oscar Wilde

SECRETS

There are decisions to make about who has what information in a piece of dialogue. Tensions can be created by realizing that one character knows things the other doesn't. Characters know things that they don't know the others already know – and so on. The listener should want to intervene, to shake a character and say, 'But she didn't mean that... but he already knows that!'

Never give your characters the same amount of information, unless it's a play about mind readers. A lot of the drama between people is caused by misunderstanding, misinterpretation and withheld information.

THE POWER OF SILENCE

Silence is often a way that people, even very articulate people, signal their disagreement with someone more than just by using speech. For example:

ANNIE   People don't always leap straight in to an argument.

  SILENCE

ANNIE   Don't you think that's right?

  SILENCE

ANNIE   Jack, are you even listening to me?
JACK   I'm thinking.
ANNIE   Well?

  SILENCE

ANNIE   Jack?
JACK   OK, OK, I expect you're right, it's just you're being really bossy.

SILENCE

JACK   Annie?

SILENCE

JACK   Look I didn't mean to hurt your feelings.
ANNIE   Well, you have, so shut up and just do as I say.

And so on.

It is also worth remembering that people don't talk articulately all the time, even highly articulate people. Being self-conscious or distressed may limit their ability to find the words for their feelings. The fact that someone usually fluent and witty suddenly runs out of words lets us know the strength of the emotion they're feeling. Or someone talking unnecessarily tells us they are nervous, lying, desperate to impress or heading out of control.

If there is something emotional to be said, it is often better to give it to the person least involved in the scene. They will babble and blurt out their feelings clumsily in a way that might sound melodramatic from the actual victim. Consider manoeuvring an emotional scene so that the least likely person tells us what's going on. Put the person with the more predictable emotions into a situation where they have to act counter to their feelings, thus heightening our awareness of their pain.

In the following scene from Sue Teddern's play *Picking Up The Pieces*, Emma is returning to work after her husband was killed in a brutal attack by street robbers. Emma is the one who doesn't tell us anything. From where this scene comes in the play, we already know why Keri is increasingly hysterical when she sees Emma. Emma's stoic silence becomes one of the most powerful forces in the dialogue.

SCENE 2   INT. STAFF KITCHEN

**JUST OFF THE MAIN OFFICE. KERI AND EMMA
COME INTO THE NEW KITCHEN.**

1 **KERI**   ...and I'm on this diet thing so I warm up my own stuff. Low-cal soup mostly. Mina does microwave chips. By the shed-load. Honestly, she eats like a horse and she's still a size 8. While I'm like practically starving myself to lose half an ounce. It's so not fair. And I've started power-walking round the industrial park every other lunchtime. Even when it's pouring with rain. I hate it.

2 **EMMA**   The kitchen's nice. Shaker style, isn't it.

3 **KERI**   My sister's got the same one in Buttermilk. Ian reckons it's a good sign, a state of the art kitchen. He says it means the company's doing really well despite the recession. (**BEAT**) Ooh, he had this massive row with Geoff last week. About projected

figures for the next quarter. Honestly, you could hear everything, even though the door was closed. But then Geoff's been in a strop ever since he split up with Becky from Sales. Or had that happened before ... um—?

4 **EMMA** — you can say it.

5 **KERI** You're so brave to come back. After everything. God, if it had been me, I'd have— (**BURSTS INTO TEARS**) I meant to phone you, Em, honestly. So many times. But I thought, you know, you needed time by yourself. With your thoughts and your family and stuff. I organised the flowers from the office. And the card. Everyone was upset. Even Geoff. (**PROPER CRYING NOW**) Oh Emma, it's so horrible.

6 **EMMA** (**HUGS HER**) Hey, it's okay. How about a cup of tea? I'll put the kettle on.

(Excerpt from *Picking Up The Pieces* by Sue Teddern)

CHARACTERS WHO DO NOTHING

Plays can have characters just talking in a vacuum. Beckett is the obvious example. There are rises and falls of tension in his dialogue, expectations raised and confounded, glimpses of character revealed. There is no spare word; no flabby moment. The drama is stripped to the bare bones. It is one of the hardest things to do.

If you want to write a play stripped bare like this, the best thing to do is to look at Beckett's plays. How much is revealed in tiny lines of dialogue, how do moods shift and crises build then dissipate? There is a drive to know something, to communicate something. Sometimes it feels we are urging someone speaking a foreign language to get the right words out and tell us what we desperately want to know about them. It is not just voices talking on and on without rhythm or reason.

CHARACTERS WHO DO SOMETHING

In a more conventional play, this one I'm inventing about Linda and her mother Jane for instance, we create atmosphere, tension and a sense of reality by getting the characters to do something. But don't have them doing something for the sake of it as this just wastes time.

If Linda wants to confront her mother about the finances, don't have her say, 'Mum, I'm making some coffee, I need us to sit down and have a talk.' The coffee serves no purpose except to waste a lot of time with characters saying 'Milk?' 'Sugar?' 'Here you are,' etc. If we were watching it, how interesting would it be? If the coffee is made and sparks the confrontation, then it is useful.

People meeting to have a conversation over meals is one of my particular *bêtes noires*. Let's say that Linda is meeting her mother for lunch and we join them in the restaurant. What purpose does the restaurant serve except to provide background noise? Will there be a lot of time wasted with waiters and ordering?

In studio, actors eat soft foods, usually bananas, so they don't choke while eating and acting. Yet they are putting in the extra work of banana eating and acting, so they like the listener to know about it. This means whenever characters are having a meal in a play, they are almost inevitably people who chew whilst speaking – and it applies from middle class matrons to medieval warlords. To me this is just irritating and unpleasant to hear. Unless the characters are going to have an argument about bad table manners.

If the medieval warlords are going to fall out and challenge each other to a duel because someone has served a forbidden food as an insult, then the meal might have a point.

If one character wants to have a heart-to-heart with another, consider finding somewhere more interesting than just a restaurant. If it's a very fancy restaurant and one of the characters is made uncomfortable, then there's a purpose. If they see their husband with another woman across the room, then there could be a purpose.

Think hard about why you're setting a scene in a particular location. Is whatever the characters are doing there going to contribute more than sound effects and banana-poisoned actor?

DIALOGUE FROM ACTION

Two people work in an office and fall in love. He can't work the computer; she comes over to help him. They have something to be doing, we know they are awkwardly close together and we learn something about their characters. Is he a man perfectly happy for a woman to be more capable or is he embarrassed? Is she a contented computer geek or is she wary of seeming a geek? Is she tactful or bossy? Where's the moment where small talk and computer instruction shifts into something more personal?

Whatever the characters are doing should contribute to the story. What they are doing can be the main subject but allow the subtext, such as 'I quite fancy you', to emerge.

Or the action can be the subtext. Perhaps a boyfriend is teaching his girlfriend to drive and has decided this is the moment to ask her to move in with him. He's talking but is constantly drawn back to the action that provides tension and establishes how they talk to each other when not in a heightened romantic moment. He's trying to declare his love but also telling her to stop crunching the gears. She's telling him she'll move in but why can't she just buy an automatic? As there's more than one topic, we don't know what way the conversation will go. What will end up the dominant theme? Will there be an argument or will love conquer bad coordination?

Keep thinking about what the character would be doing that tells us more about them. Will what they are doing make the dialogue full of different layers and shifting emotions?

If the characters are at work, how competent and dedicated to the work are they? Does their busyness make them abrupt in the conversation or are they eager to slow down for a talk?

The important thing is to keep characters active while they're talking. Even if they are Beckett-style characters in a wilderness, they will still do things such as see something that distracts them, or imagine they hear someone coming. They have things to do as well as just talk.

Action doesn't have to be energetic. Sometimes characters are simply lying in bed at the end of the day worrying about what might happen tomorrow. This can be done in dramatic rather than passive ways. You could have one character say, 'Well goodnight, love, I hope we manage to sleep instead of lying awake worrying.' It is far better to skip ahead an hour, then have character sit up and say, 'I can't sleep,' and have the other agree. Then they can discuss what's tormenting them, but we've already shown in action that they're tormented. Their dialogue now doesn't have to be overloaded with explained emotion.

If your characters are doing nothing much, is the scene the most dramatic way of depicting their situation?

What characters are doing while they are talking can reveal character, plot, mood and atmosphere. Try to think about what they are doing as much as you would think about the action in a film. In radio there is less action to go with the dialogue, so it needs to work harder.

In a film, a man is driving a tank; we can see he is nervous, sweating, but trying to talk about lap dancers with his mates. The same scene can happen on radio; there just needs to be some indication in the dialogue that he has more on his mind than lap dancers, some carefully chosen hesitation or sudden aside. Think of a line that would have the same effect as showing us that he is secretly sweating buckets.

Strangely, the thing I like is the very thing that deterred me from radio drama initially, having come straight from Rep, where I had fought to get a rehearsal period up to five weeks, terrifying then going to no rehearsal at all, as such. But I have found this to be liberating and there is a sense of the script as the whole thing. Get the casting right and it can work its own magic, with my role as more editorial rather than in leading interpretation. Everything you need to know about the character is on the page. Or should be. I am a great believer in 'you are how you speak, as much as you are what you say'. Syntax is my first reference when determining who the character is. Actors know that punctuation isn't random, it is a mirror reflection of how the character thinks, and how they think is who they are.

Marina Calderone, independent director and radio producer

WHO IS TALKING

If the people in the scene are different ages, male and female, from different places, it is much easier to know who is talking than if they are all young people of the same sex. Older actors have more distinctive voices. Two older people will have developed their tones and quirks of speech even without adding in an accent. After a few moments listening, we can tell Bill Nighy from Michael Gambon; we can tell Joanna Lumley from Penelope Wilton.

With younger actors, the voices are less developed and can sound similar. If four characters in a play are nineteen-year-old soldiers it's worth thinking about giving them different accents. What if it's essential to the story that they are all from Liverpool? Then it's doubly important to think if one is quiet-spoken, one bombastic, one cheeky and one a born misery. The characteristics of their way of speaking is in the writer's hands. Finding voices that sound as different as possible in a narrow parameter is a job for the producer but not entirely. Even on paper, four nineteen-year-olds from the same street in Liverpool will not speak in the same way.

Wondering how listeners will know who is talking often preoccupies writers new to radio. Think of all the people you know, around your age. How often do you confuse them when you hear them on the phone? Perhaps only occasionally in the first few moments of conversation.

In a play we will know who is talking if you have made their way of talking distinctive and characterful, and if everything they say in a scene serves a purpose for their character.

WHAT DOES IT SOUND LIKE?

It's really hard to know if your dialogue is working without trying it out. Try a rough approximation of how you imagine the characters will sound – even if you are the worst actor on earth, it will help you hear if a line sounds appropriate, fluid or necessary.

Reading the scene aloud and attempting to act it out will give you an idea if someone is talking for too long, or if the whole conversation goes on too long. Hearing your own lines helps you to know if they are tongue-twisters. Hearing your lines will help you hear if they sound written, rather than sounding like effortlessly natural speech.

> I said 'a line will take us hours maybe,
> Yet if it does not seem a moment's thought
> Our stitching and unstitching has been naught.'
> From 'Adam's Curse' by W.B. Yeats, 1904

PEOPLE ARE LISTENING

Another thing to bear in mind when writing dialogue is that people are listening to each other. Are they listening to each other with interest or with impatience? Are there reasons, due to character or situation, why they would interrupt? Where characters interrupt, a clear way to indicate this is to write out the whole sentence. This way the actor know where the line is going and can put the right emotion into a half-sentence. They can continue until they feel the interruption has come in naturally, rather than stopping dead in mid air.

For example:

JANE   I can't wait, my car's...(on a meter)

LINDA **(INTERRUPTING)** You have to listen to this, you can't keep pretending everything's OK.

JANE   I know its not OK, but talking won't help.

LINDA Listening to some advice might... (help you)

JANE   **(INTERRUPTING)** I can't get a ticket.

LINDA When will you be home?

JANE   I don't know, it's difficult to... (say when)

LINDA **(INTERRUPTING)** Then I'm coming with you.

Don't leave lines hanging because the actors may not know what you intend.

When people interrupt each other they overlap; each person wants to finish their sentence and often do, but they just get drowned out. If you listen to radio plays often, you will hear terrible moments where characters are supposed to be interrupting but the overlap isn't made clear so we get melo-dramatic sounding gaps.

DIALOGUE CHECKLIST

1. Is the character doing something while they talk?
2. How does the character talk?
3. Are they saying something appropriate to their character?
4. Do they need to have the conversation at all?
5. How many things are going on in the conversation. Do we have plot, character, tension and mood, as well as banter and philosophical points being put across?
6. When a dialogue scene is finished read it aloud.
7. After reading, see what words you don't need in the dialogue, shave it down, then read it again. Maybe shave it again or replace mere chatter with something revealing of character or plot.

5 MONOLOGUES

THE SAME RULES APPLY

Some very effective radio plays are pure monologues. These are much harder to write than they might seem; think of the difference between riding a bicycle and riding a unicycle.

In a monologue, someone is telling a story. This is very different to a reading. Think of Alan Bennett's *Talking Heads*. These monologues are active, often in the present tense. We have a sense that the character is making the story up as they go along. We have a sense that they are piecing the facts together for themselves. As they remember things, or think of things they hadn't realized before, the story remains fresh, active.

We could watch someone for this length of time, doing different things, see their facial expression change, or see them go to intriguing places, but we wouldn't have the wonderful sense of being told a story.

If we read a narration in a book we imagine the voice changing, imagine the shifts of tone. In radio this work is done for us. Radio is more work than television and less than reading.

Writing monologue requires a real relish for storytelling, a gifted ear for the strange things people say and a powerful sense of rhythm. Where does the direction of the monologue need to shift so that the listener's attention is rebooted? Where does the pace need to shift to prevent monotony?

A play could be one long monologue, or a collection of them juxtaposed, or monologues could be broken up with remembered dialogue within them. Perhaps the characters for various reasons can't communicate, even though they are side by side.

In the excerpt below, one character is immobile in a hospital bed, the other is at the bedside. The scene shifts to the places that the characters are thinking of, then back to the hospital to remind us why they are all connected at this moment, as well as in life in general. The characters can't communicate but reveal themselves to have intense reasons to piece together information about each other, to remember why they ended up in hospital together.

There is a third character, a nurse observing the situation. The nurse has problems of her own. She doesn't communicate with the others because she likes to keep a professional distance, despite her curiosity. Yet eventually she is drawn in to participate in the story.

We are inside these characters' heads. Their thoughts are what we follow. We are trying to piece together the facts and meanings with the characters. This intimate and direct style of writing works well on radio but all the rules about holding the listener's interest intensify.

SCENE TWO. INT. CARA'S HOUSE. 11.00AM

1.**CARA:** I'd nearly finished the body and I was just about to start on the wings when I saw it. The dead mouse. Under the coffee table. It freaked me out. I couldn't deal with it. So I went back to working on the swan, hoping that when I turned back again the mouse would run off or just not be there. It was about as optimistic as hoping my dolls and teddies would talk to each other when I left them alone when I was a kid. Eventually I made myself prop open the front door. I'd put on five carrier bags, two on each hand and one on my head cos it had started to rain. So then all I needed to do was scoop it up and run unimpeded to the dustbin. I kept telling myself it would only take a few seconds and it would be over.

FX: FRONT DOOR IS OPEN. RAIN. TRAFFIC MASKS THE SOUND OF ELAINE COMING IN.

2 **CARA:** I had one last look to memorize its position so I could bend down and grab it with my eyes closed when I felt a presence in the room – behind me – I turned round and there she was – Elaine. Only I didn't know her name then. I thought she'd just wandered in off the street, that she was a patient on day release from the psychiatric unit down the road. She looked so weird just standing staring at me I didn't want to be too like 'get out of my house' but I really, really didn't want her in it. I felt scared and then guilty for feeling scared.

How much time in my life have I wasted on guilt? How much of my life have I wasted? Why am I thinking that now? Why do I have to think that? You don't have to. Make yourself try and remember what happened next.

3.**ELAINE:** You see, at first I thought Cara was a nutter or maybe a burglar. All those carrier bags. The place looked mad. There were enormous, half-finished papier-mâché things everywhere, glitter, chicken wire and feathers like a comic book illustration of a pillow fight. I was dumbstruck. It was (**CONTINUES**)

(**CONTINUES**) only later I learnt that she was a prop maker. But at the time I was thrown for a loop. I'd worked myself up to this moment. I had it all planned, my razor sharp articulate, slice-to-the-bone speech, my cold, hard, stare but then it all went pear-shaped. I just stood there, a vision of gormlessness. I couldn't believe my husband had run off with her. I just couldn't. To say she is no oil painting is, well she's no watercolour or pastel or crayoning. Not even any make-up. So pale, hair cropped so close that it could have only been done in the barbers. Or with sandpaper. Big baggy boiler suit on. Aged forty in 2004! It was only afterwards I realized it was her work clothes. Even so. Even so. No wonder I was speechless. It was incredible, impossible! Because let me tell you I haven't been married to him for twenty-five years not to know the type he goes for and it has never included flat-chested, nail-biting, virtually bald, waifs. But then I reminded myself, he's not getting any younger so he can't be as picky as he used to be. And I'd got this far. I knew this was the house. He'd been here every week for the past few months. He doesn't know I know. He never does. I stalk him. I always do that. As long as I know where he is, it calms me. Makes me feel I'm one step ahead. Ha. I'd never actually seen her before, though. I'd had to be careful not to get caught. Now he'd broken every unspoken rule we'd silently negotiated – and left me. Only I wasn't prepared just to let him go, not with all we've been through, not without – Well, actually – not at all. It's just not an option. So I said as levelly as I could to the bit of scrag end in the boiler-suit that I would like to talk to my husband. She might look like she's completely bloody thick but she seemed to grasp the situation quicker than I did. 'D'you mean Terry?' I nodded confirmation. As if I might have two husbands or something. Huh, I should be so unlucky. 'He's not here' she said quite lev-elly. Then 'He's now living with my partner.' 'Ex partner.' She said correcting herself without batting an unadorned eyelid. (**LOSES IT**) Oh now let me tell you my husband's sexual preferences are by no (**CONTINUES**)

(**CONTINUES**)means fussy. I was even pared to believe he'd been having an affair with her. But with a MAN? Terry??? Terry going in for sex without breasts? Unthinkable. Maybe this bloke was one of those 'lady-boys' you see on documentaries on Channel Five. While my mind was racing at a million miles an hour in the wrong direction my legs buckled beneath me and I had no choice but to sit down. And as I did so I took in the mouse under the table, and on a peripheral level put that together with the carrier bags.
That must have been what she was about to do when I walked in – getting rid of the mouse. Then I took a proper look at her. I looked at her through the eyes of those girls who do that programme 'What Not To Wear' and they'd say, 'Why do you dress like that, you look like a billiard playing bar dyke.' And then the penny smacked me in the face. Of course she does because that's exactly what she is. Her partner must have been – is – a woman. And then the world was back in reality – sense was made. Of course. Of course, that would be a fantasy come true for Tez – that would be the dream topping on the conquest cake – to go to bed with a lesbian.

(Excerpt from *Partial Eclipse Of The Heart* by Sarah Daniels)

The ground is constantly shifting in these monologues. We are following Cara, then Elaine makes us wonder if Cara is reliable. We have vivid pictures of people and places, descriptions that also add to character and plot. Other characters are mentioned, building the world of the play. There are apparent digressions but all the while, the story is moving on.

WHEN MONOLOGUE IS GOOD

Setting limitations such as using monologue could be useful for a student production. If you were trying to create drama on the cheap, to put on the internet for instance, this is a useful form – limited actors and effects, clear edit points. The limitations mean that the quality of the writing and performance have to be exceptional. They should always be exceptional of course but the more limited the form, the more impatient and minute the scrutiny from the listener.

Good monologues can work brilliantly. Gary Oldman's performance in *Walk Right By Me* is one of the most powerful pieces of radio I have ever experienced. Lee Hall's extraordinary, award-winning play about faith, love and the meaning of life is another classic monologue. Both characters, speaking directly to the listener, are compelling and vivid. But this is due, partly to brilliant performances, but largely to the strength of the writing. Too often writers use monologue as a lazy radio drama device. ('If I have this character talking directly to the audience, it saves me having to dramatize the situation.') Plays that, five scenes in, suddenly have a character speaking his or her intimate thoughts, rarely convince.

Gordon House, former Head of BBC World Service Drama

WHEN MONOLOGUE IS BAD

'I get sent too many monologues by new writers. They don't make them dramatic. It's just prose,' one radio producer complained to me. Radio producers generally seem to feel that writers underestimate how active a monologue has to be to hold attention.

Radio readings such as *A Book at Bedtime* never last more than around twelve minutes. This is a long time to listen to a single voice. There is usually a great book being read, but see how often your attention wanders even in this short space of time. Then imagine how to hold the listener's attention for forty-five minutes or more with a single voice.

It's worth studying the scripts of good monologues – Alan Bennett, Harold Pinter, Beckett, Sebastian Barry or Debbie Tucker Green. These are very different writers who all know how to keep a talking head alive.

All the rules of radio drama apply of course – questions have to be asked, characters have to be believable, and their words sound as though they come from them. The listener still has to wonder what's happening, and what's going to happen next. A good story isn't enough; you need to have great storytelling skills. Monologue writing needs to be a deft and concise as dialogue writing. Are you writing a monologue because dialogue seems too limiting? Doesn't this mean that you think the way people speak is limiting? Perhaps prose would be a better medium.

The secret of being a bore... is to tell everything.

On the Nature of Man, Voltaire, 1737

LETTERS AND EMAILS

A number of very effective radio plays have been written using collection of real or imagined correspondence. These are short juxtaposed monologues. They create involving drama by allowing the listener to join in, piecing together the story. Letters and email give a logic to the monologues – we know who the characters are addressing and why they are addressing them.

Letters tend to be considered; emails hasty. Emails are the closest to dialogue because people blurt things out, misunderstand and don't always form elegant sentences. Letters written by people who aren't articulate in speech can be quite funny, or quite sad. People tend to adopt a formality in letter writing, they feel they have to strain to be more eloquent. It might be an interesting exercise to try creating a short drama, say fifteen minutes, composed of letters between two people who aren't used to writing letters. Why are they doing this? What are they trying to say to each other? How much are their situations changing in between letters.

Exchanges of letters and emails are like writing scenes. Some need to be short, some longer. Their emotional tone needs to change from one piece of correspondence to the next. Or the tone escalates – angry, angrier, angriest. Depression descending to despair on one side, while the other starts trying to be cheering and becomes impatient, then depressed themselves. Each letter should contain surprises. And all the time, the story needs to keep moving forward.

6 SCENERY AND ACTION

CHANGING LOCATIONS

In plays that can change location, there should be more chances to keep the listener interested. The listener is unsettled: we're here, now we're there – what's going on? Changing locations, however, can also just irritate the listener if the change is happening as a cheat. If the play asks no questions, has no tension, then leaping from desert Island, to boardroom, to ocean liner won't change this.

Each scene, however tiny, has to contain its own mini-story. There should be tension within the scene. What are the characters going to do or say next? How much more of the story will be revealed? Will there be more surprises?

The scene should not outstay its welcome. It should end while the listener is still enjoying it. We should leave the desert island for the boardroom still fascinated with what was happening on the island.

Changing scenes should have a purpose. If we were in the kitchen, have we finished with the kitchen business? Or are we moving to the garden simply to have a change of background noise while we continue the same kitchen conversation? Perhaps the kitchen conversation is going on a long time. Perhaps it is interrupted by a gale of wind and the bins blowing over outside. The characters have to go, deal with the crisis and continue their conversation in a gale force wind, covered in slimy rubbish. This may make them more irritated; it may bond them. Not only has the scenery changed but the mood has changed.

Characters shouldn't move for no real reason but bear in mind that a scene that lasts more than two pages is getting to be a long scene. Yet it may be a great scene, intense and riveting; moving it elsewhere would break the tension. In this case, don't move yet. Perhaps the characters have become as angry as they can be in the kitchen – they need a change to get worse or to dissolve into laughter, as it turns out that tackling wet rubbish and fighting bitterly doesn't work.

What is going on in the scene should suggest that it's time to move; it may need to be shifted to up the ante, change the dynamic or dissipate a mood.

WHERE TO GO?

Your play may all be set in one house. Let's say that for some reason the characters can't go outside. How do we know what room we're in? We could waste time with a lot of coming in and out of doors so we know people are changing rooms. Sometimes door action may be necessary. Mostly it wastes time.

Perhaps a couple in a house are being held hostage. There is a kidnapper in the kitchen and one in the hall at the front door. Kitchens and halls have different sounds. So do bathrooms. Perhaps the couple is supposed to stay in the living room with the curtains drawn. There are also sofas, carpets, armchairs in the living room – creating a softer sound.

The furnishings in different rooms make different sounds. Is one room near a road, and the other near a garden? Is there a fridge noise in the kitchen? Is there a noisy clock in the living room? It's important not to get too bogged down in worrying about this, rooms sound different, that's all you need to know. Studio technicians are great at creating different sounds for different rooms. It is up to the writer to think about why the characters are moving from room to room.

Making tea in the kitchen – that's obvious. But perhaps a violent scene would be better in a bathroom than bedroom – the floors are hard, the listener can imagine more heavy fittings and sharp edges. Do the kidnappers drag their captives into the bathroom there because it will be easier to clean the blood? If you consider the atmosphere you want for the scene, the reason the people moving from place to place, you'll always be helped with the technical side of achieving the sound of different rooms. If you have scenes placed with no logic or purpose, the sound effects are wasted. If listeners are thinking, 'That must be the living room, there's that noisy clock again,' then they can't be very absorbed in the dialogue and the story.

MANAGING THE PEOPLE

The characters can be in different rooms and different groups. One kidnapper and two hostages; all four characters; two kidnappers; another kidnapper and two hostages and so on.

To create a varied texture in scenes, it's worth checking that you don't have two people talking, followed by two people talking, followed by another scene of two people talking. Perhaps you are deliberately creating a pattern of duologues; in this case they will need to have a very different dynamic within them – a father and son; the son and his girlfriend; the girlfriend and her father; the two fathers. You have very different groupings of voice to create texture.

As discussed in the dialogue chapter, pace and tone will also create a play with texture. An angry scene, followed by a happy scene, followed by an angry scene then a peaceful meditative moment, and so on. Changing the way the people are behaving and talking creates a different kind of scene as much as changing location.

SHAPE OF THE SCENE

Are the people in a big room or a small room? Are they close together? In studio, microphones can be positioned to indicate that people are in different parts of a large room. Similarly, everything will be closed down around one microphone if people are trapped in a cupboard under the stairs together.

This is another way to create different textures between scenes. The rooms people move into don't have to be dramatically different, but where they are in relation to each other in the room can create a difference in the type of conversation they have.If the couple being held hostage are tied together, their conversation will sound very different to two kidnappers talking across a large kitchen.

It's also worth remembering that people talk as they walk. If a kidnapper has been in the hall whispering with another kidnapper, he may see the hostages are whispering, plotting something in the living room. He walks as he yells at them to stop whispering. Then he is in the living room, having another conversation with a different dynamic, while the second kidnapper follows him in, also talking as he walks. We have two static conversations broken up with two on the move. We have some texture.

MIXING ACTION AND STILLNESS

In the scene later in this chapter from the play *On The Field*, there are comfortable monologues interrupted by violent scenes where there are several characters and confusing events. There are contrasts of tone in the opening scenes of this play but also several stories are being introduced. The listeners have to hold the trivial plot of the monologues in their head, while wondering what is going on in the field of battle. They have to piece together the connections between the monologues and the people in the battle.

There is quiet with the monologues and noise with the battle. The monologue is like the close-up shot in a film; the battle is like the crowd scene. We hear Julie and her concerns clearly and obviously. The crowd of the battle is almost out of focus it is so agitated and busy.

THINK FILM

Think about the geography of scenes as if you are composing shots for a film. People need to hear different sorts of sound and dialogue, the way they need to look at different things to keep them stimulated and attentive. In *On the Field* it is easy to see what the director's list of shots might be if it were a film script – the close up on Julie, then the camera pulled back for the group in battle. Or perhaps we see Julie at a distance, across a quiet room and jump to distorted close-up of a soldier in battle. Writing radio drama is about these same minute decisions.

Sometimes a film is about smaller shifts in focus, all set in one room with two characters. Returning to *Poisoned By a Tree* on page 28, if it were a film we would change shots to be with Barbara at the window, then perhaps there'd be a shot of the airship, then there'd be the two women together, then there'd be a close up of Sarah's face as her pain emerges, then back to a shot of the two of women as Barbara returns to jokey mood.

In radio you have words and sounds to help the audience decide where the focus is, when they can see a whole room and when there's a close up. And all the time they should be asking – what is that noise? Who is that? What are they doing? Why are they doing it? And most importantly, what is going to happen next? What happens next could be a shell exploding or a telephone ringing. What happens next could be the words of a character like Julie changing the direction of the play. It looks as though we're headed into tragedy but there is this nagging domesticity, this comic aside to consider. Perhaps this isn't a serious play about war. Or perhaps Julie's trivial comfort will be shattered by the harsh realities of war.

Questions, questions....

1   EXT   ARMY CAMP BASRA DAY

> **SOUND OF ROCKET/MORTAR FIRE DISTANT THEN SUDDENLY CLOSE AND VERY LOUD.**
>
> **SOUND TO BACKGROUND**

JULIE   (VOICE OVER) Dear Craig, I know it must be all go in Iraq but in our own way we've had much excitement here. The radiator in the back bedroom, you know the one that's always been leaking....? Well our Helen and I got back from our short break in Lanzarote to find utter disaster.

> **SOUND OF ROCKET/MORTAR FIRE LOUD**

BILLY   Incoming! This way. Move!

> **SOUND OF HEAVY FEET RUNNING IN SAND**

BILLY   Here. Down, get down!

> **SCUFFLING. SOLDIERS ARE CROUCHING BEHIND SANDBAGS**

CRAIG   Where are they?
BILLY   Over there, maybe over there... Never you mind nosy parker, get your head down.

> **ROCKET FIRE CLOSE THEN TO BACKGROUND**

JULIE   (VOICE OVER) After all the months of leaking, the thing had suddenly burst, water all down the front room, sideboard ruined... Mercifully I've been conscientious with the insurance.

> **ROCKET FIRE CLOSE**

CRAIG   Shouldn't we get under better cover?
BILLY   Aye, maybe get to one of the reinforced bunkers.
DAVE   Maybe definitely.

BILLY   The only bunkers here are in your brains son, just sit tight, we're as good behind here as anywhere, welcome to Basra.

ROCKETS CONTINUE. A SIREN BEGINS THEN BOTH SOUNDS FADE UNDER.

JULIE   (VOICE OVER) Luckily there's no damage on the other side of the room, so the flat screen is safe for watching the quarter final, or our Helen would be in bits. Speaking of which, there's a big spread in OK magazine about the house Sean Byrne's had built in Cheshire. They say he's had trouble with some tendon but he's fit again now. Which brings me to say, although I know you said you didn't want any fusspot talk, but just once I'd like to say be safe son, being there's brave enough without any extra.

SIREN TRAILS OFF

(Excerpt from *On the Field* by Annie Caulfield)

Where You Can't Go

They say you can go anywhere you like in radio. This isn't quite true. In *On the Field*, any battle scenes were deliberately short because it's very hard with a half dozen actors rolling around a studio floor to create the atmosphere of battle, however many sound effects are thrown in. The trick is to create an impression and get out of the scene fast.

Later in this play there's a football match. We stole from the film *Zidane* by having microphones on the players as they ran, creating distortion, picking up heavy breathing. We are with the players as they shout to each other and run, there's only a few moments of this, giving the impression of an energetic, chaotic amateur match.

Radio does not do large action scenes well. It doesn't do crowd scenes well. Half a dozen actors in a studio running and shouting never sounds like a riot. Even if sound effects are built behind the live sound, there's always a sense of artificiality. Better to go deliberately for the artificial, the impressionistic, the stylized.

In a play I wrote about peace marches and riots in Northern Ireland, we had some real news footage of rioting. We cut this in with a woman talking about how their peace movement was growing despite the attacks. With the sound of the riots and the woman's voice, we had the sound of one woman's feet on a pavement in the foreground, then a second set of feet, then a third – with the half dozen people in the studio we suggested a building crowd. Then the real sound of the riot overwhelmed the walking sound, to signify the attacks on the marchers.

The Intimate in the Epic

Radio scenes are intimate. They can be an intimate kernel in an epic story. For instance, if the film *Lawrence of Arabia's* opening scene were the start of a radio play, you might have two Arab boys minding goats and speculating about the figure riding in from the distance. We can move as quickly from the boys in the desert to the British command in Jerusalem as we could in the film. What will sound messy is a battle scene. Better to find a symbol of battle – a single burst of machine gun fire and a scream. Think about how the battle would sound to one person rather than hope for a panoramic battle sound.

Contrasts of Place

Two people could be having the most fascinating discussion about military strategy in the Iraq war, but that is just two people talking; it isn't a play. We might listen to the discussion with intellectual interest but a drama has to provoke our emotional interest and our curiosity. There is no sense of what is going to happen next in even the most vibrant discussions.

The minute you feel your characters have settled into a mere discussion, interrupt them with a new character coming into the room, a change of scene or a new physical problem they have to solve.

If you feel the characters started discussing something important that needs to be elucidated further, make room for the end of the discussion later. If the discussion starts in a war zone, have it conclude in a bar or vice versa. Doing this, the way they discuss the topic will change too. It can shift from fevered to considered. It could become ironic.

As a rule of thumb characters should discuss war in a bar and types of beer in a war. The scene will always be livelier if the words and atmosphere don't match.

Contrasts of Movement

If two characters are hiking across a desert, we should hear that one is tired before they say, 'I'm tired.' Hearing how people move is another way to add to character and story. If a character comes into a street walking briskly, their story will be very different to one that we hear shuffling.

Listening, we may not pick up on the creaks of a comfortable armchair but we will hear it in the leisurely way a character talks. If they are sitting cross-legged on the floor, they will, most likely, be more alert and sharper in the way they speak. If a character is sitting comfortably, remember that their way of talking will change once they stand up. An uncomfortable character will be in more of a hurry to move on, or at least less eager to linger.

Imagining how characters are moving will help you build a fuller picture of them. If there is a reason why they are moving in a certain way – they're tired, they are hiding, they're in a hurry – they don't have to explain themselves right away. A change in tone of voice can create an intrigue for a few moments, then they can drop a line into the conversation that explains what's happening to them.

Remember, characters draw the curtains before they say, 'I'll draw the curtains.' They walk slowly and heavily before they say, 'I'm tired.'

DON'T FORGET PEOPLE

If you have four people having a conversation in a room, do they all need to be there? The problem with radio is that we only know if people are there if they are speaking. Unless we've established that one is in a coma on a life support machine, in which case we'll hear their machine and know they haven't miraculously wandered off.

If you have four people, they all need to say something once in a while to remind the listener they are there. So if they have one important line and then say, 'I agree with George' later on, do they need to be there?

An actor I left stranded with no lines for most of a scene volunteered to cough occasionally to let people know he was still there. I'd written him in to the scene and he had important things to say at the start but then he just hung around while two other characters arguing, saying; 'Yes, let's go' when his ally decides to leave. There was nothing useful for him to say in the middle of the scene, so we quickly wrote in a line for him to leave on after his important lines, along with a good reason for him to be leaving of course.

Similarly, you could have four people in a scene and person four doesn't speak until about eight lines in. This is very disconcerting for the listener – where did they spring from?

Do all the characters need to be in the scene? If so, remember that if they're not speaking we wonder where they've gone.

For dull budgetary reasons, writers are urged to keep cast sizes small. This can actually help clear out anyone non-essential. In a building site foreman's office, for instance, he is discussing plans with the architect. On television he would probably have a non-speaking secretary in the background. There are no non-speaking secretaries in radio, and no need for secretaries who just say, 'There's an urgent phone call from your wife, Mr Jones.'

Have Mr Jones answer his own phone. If the absence of a secretary worries you, have Mr Jones tell the architect to excuse him for a moment, that his secretary is sick, he has to answer the call... Or just don't mention a secretary – people will wonder about her if she's mentioned, and won't think about it if she's not.

Strip scenes down to the minimum number of people required. In a bar, have the people with their drink, already in mid conversation. Don't have a barman unless he's going to interrupt the conversation by setting himself on fire. Don't allow people in your play who just take up lines and aren't characters. Will the barman say more than, 'Do you want ice sir?' If he doesn't, then he's not earning his keep.

> What I hate in a script? Exposition. Assumptions about the audience.
> Information. Scenes that go nowhere. Cliché. Narrators who don't know who
> they're talking to. Second hand wit. Characters who talk to themselves
> without reason. Characters who talk to each other without reason.
> Characters who tell each other anything they both know they both know.
> Talkers without character. Time specific secondary directions (e.g. 'she holds
> her breath for twenty seconds').
>
> Jessica Dromgoole, BBC drama producer

WHO'S THAT MAN

Another pet hate among interviewed producers is a tendency among first-time
writers to send in scripts where characters have no names. They are listed as
'MAN ONE', 'MAN TWO'. Or 'BOY' and 'GIRL'. This is something that makes
hearts sink. It may be intended as minimalist but it usually suggests that Man
One, Man Two, Boy and Girl have no characters – they just have lines.

The minute you start to think about a name for a character, you start to
think about the sort of person they are. Is the character called George? No?
George doesn't suit him? Why not? He's young, from Tottenham, George does-
n't feel like the right name for him... Already Man One is becoming more than
a cipher.

Even a character speaking the most minimal, inarticulate or mysterious
dialogue is a whole person.

Actors also hate to glance though a script and see they have been allocated
'Man One'. They mind the tiny role less if the character is a George or a Sean.
A name gives them a building block to start with.

If the character is someone who shouts a line of abuse at the lead character in the street and goes on their way, at least call him 'Shouting Man'.
Have a picture of who he is in your head – is he a skinhead, a drunk, a
concerned citizen? Better to call him that then. He has a semi-formed iden-
tity that will show in the words he chooses to shout. After all, even Daleks
have names.

WHAT ACTION WORKS

Speaking of Daleks, frightening things work well on the radio. We've all been
scared by a creak on the stairs at home. We're alone in the house, is there
something there?

On television we can see the Daleks coming and take fright. The thing is,
once a Dalek is there, you're pretty much dead. On radio we can hear their
terrible voices coming from far away and build the fear for much longer.

> Present fears are less than horrible imaginings.
>
> William Shakespeare. *Macbeth*, Act I, scene iii

Fear in real life is a product of our imagination. We hear something creak and imagine the most terrifying kind of intruder to us. For a child it would be a monster; for an adult it might be a man with an axe or a crack addict with a knife. On radio we are with the character who hears the noise. We are imagining our own worst fears, so have moments of personal fright that no one can script. We're writing our own script until the monster or murderer is revealed.

People tend to listen to the radio alone. They're ripe for the scaring!

HAVE SEX ON THE RADIO WITH CAUTION

BBC Radio is still a little old-fashioned regarding swearing and sex.

If strong swear words are vital to your play and the commissioners think your play is important, a late night slot may be found for it. Although, with only words to deal with, swear words seem far more powerful on radio so a choice few can create the impact you want.

As for sex on the radio, the problem is that the sound effects can be as ludicrous and undignified as they are in real life.

> What's the hardest thing to write for the radio? Sex. It can so easily sound laughable and embarrassing. It's very difficult to make it sound right. Not as difficult as sex on stage though.
>
> Sarah Daniels, dramatist

It might be wiser, sexier and more interesting to find other ways to create an erotic scene. How do people talk to each other just before sex? Just after?

Simply the changes in breathing could be more evocative than hearing an extended spree of load moaning, groaning and chafing body parts. It may be better to think subtlety and stylization to get a genuinely sexy effect – and leave the squeaky noisy bits to the listeners' imagination. Except perhaps in a comedy.

Violence, like sex, is often better dealt with subtly on radio. Actors shrieking while studio assistants thump mattresses only sounds convincing for an instant; and seldom sounds convincing if they're trying to represent a big pub brawl rather than a one-to-one punch-up.

How can violence be portrayed subtly? A battered wife, for instance, is often broken by cruel menacing words before the beating starts. Then we'll hear the slightest sound of movement from the menacer and fear the worst.

Telling us what's happening seldom has a powerful effect. Hints of menace in words and effect will be far more chilling than shouts of, 'Please, not the baseball bat!' followed by thuds and groans. This approach sounds messy, confused – and emotion is dissipated. One good thud and groan, carefully placed after atmosphere-tensing dialogue, can be far more shocking than attempts to get a blow-by-blow representation.

If your play is full of swearing, sex and violence, but about something very important, the producers will have cleared the way for it before the recording stage. Or they will have helped you find a way to tell your story in a way that means it can be broadcast without the BBC losing it's licence fee money.

With the internet and possible new commercial markets, the lesser accountability could allow for more risky and iconoclastic radio dramas.

Again, it isn't worth pre-empting what's allowed and what isn't. If your writing is powerful but too full of knifings, cursings and casual sex for current broadcast comfort, your writing will still be what catches the producer's eye. It's their job to steer you round any obstacles of what's deemed tasteful and decent.

Using the Form

Try to think of action that could only work on radio. For example, every evening, someone comes home to a succession of scary messages on their answering machine. The world from the point-of-view of a blind person. Or the story of a great beauty – no one needs to worry who to cast.

I remember seeing a stage play about a fictional great modern painter. Characters talked about the wonderful paintings. When one was finally revealed at the end of the play, I didn't think it was all that good. On radio these issues of visual taste don't arise.

Some of the radio plays that stick in the memory are those that would only happen on radio. The writer has seen the form as an opportunity rather than a challenge.

Patricia Wood's 1991 play, *Lavender Song* was about a group of men grotesquely disfigured in World War One. At first we don't know that this is the reason for their isolated post-war lifestyle, their sad sense of being cut off from the future. Listening to their day-to-day rapport, we come to like them as individuals – there's just this nagging curiosity about why they live as they do. When a new character reacts to the disfigurement, everything falls into place. We are left to imagine how these characters we have come to know might look. We aren't ourselves distracted by wrestling with physical repugnance. We can concentrate on the emotion in this powerful story.

Researching Old Broadcasts

Finding selected old scripts and archived recordings can be done through the BBC Writers Room website. However, many are not available at the moment but it is worth checking the schedules of the digital station BBC7, where many classic plays are repeated. If you've missed something that looks interesting there is the BBC Listen again service online, free for seven days after broadcast.

Producers are very busy and with the most encouraging will in the world, aren't really able to respond to individual requests for old recordings and scripts. There are plenty of examples on the Writers Room site and new plays on every day of course...

Keep listening and imagining how a play would work on television or stage. If you can't imagine it, it's probably a good radio play.

Incidentally, pet hate near the top of pet hates among radio producers is a script accompanied by a letter saying: 'I originally wrote this for the stage/film, but thought it would work well on radio if you could give me a few pointers on how to adapt it.' This so-called 'adapting' is the radio writer's job.

7 Sound

SOUNDS IS ACTION

The sound comes before the words. It may be a sound we don't recognize, a gun being cleaned for instance. Hearing the sound is like a purely visual shot in a film. Then people talk, and a few lines in, someone says, 'Why are you cleaning your gun?' We don't need to know right away what a sound is, but don't forget to explain it at some point or it will become like the character stranded without lines. A nagging annoyance. 'What is that noise?' is asked with an irritated tone rather than curiosity.

Some sounds, such as a car engine starting, may not need explanation. It's really a matter of common sense deciding what sounds need to be explained and what will be recognizable. Mundane sounds such as a car engine will tell us that people are travelling somewhere without much need for explanation. Gun cleaning is not a common experience and requires more to be told. If it's happening in an army setting it may be a routine background noise simply requiring a mention; if it's happening in a domestic situation it is probably part of the plot.

THE SOUND OF A PLACE

Stylizing the sense of place works better on radio than trying to create a realistic picture of what the place sounds like. A beach for instance – a few seagulls and waves, we're there. An actual beach will probably have other sounds - people shouting, radios playing, cars on the promenade... The real sound is often too messy. Sounds that aren't necessary to the impression are usually cleaned out of a soundtrack to give a clear sense of the place.

If a play is set in a canteen, a real canteen may have someone in the background who has a persistent loud laugh. There may be too many people present – a busy place full of people talking can sound too much just like addled noise rather than giving a recognizable impression of a place.

There are many, many pre-recorded CDs available to technicians but they won't of course, have sound specific to your play. If for instance, you want children playing in the background, there may be a pre-recording of a playground but not four children in a garden in Ireland. High speed trains, cars starting – the sound of inanimate objects are the things it's easiest to assume will be available. Anything involving people is likely to require special recording for your play.

Children are a problem as bringing in child actors to do some background playing and laughing is an expense. It's customary to resort to having the female adult actors talking in high voices, mixing in some nature sounds and hoping it just about holds together.

Out of This World

Non-naturalistic sound pictures are easy to create on radio. If your play is about a war among Martians, the right sounds can be built in the studio. Are they made of metal? This is good, they can clang. Do they emit a high-pitched whine while when dying? Some appropriate high-pitched sound can be found.

You can build this Martian war, but be specific. Like any war, we only need a few sounds to create an impression. Then we need to know who is in the scene, what are they doing and the sound fades to the background while we focus on the story that is going on for individual Martians.

Parties and Battlefields

Too much sound soon becomes messy. It isn't anything like the scenes that can be created on film. It's just noise and we don't know what's going on storywise.

Radio can go anywhere but think hard what it's going to sound like to someone sitting alone with their radio. We want them to ask, 'What's that noise?' More than think, 'Yes, yes, a battle's going on, I get it, but what's really happening?'

Studio engineers are very experienced and innovative when it comes to getting the sound right. They will teach you a great deal simply in the questions they ask you about your script. However, it is better to be specific and keep control of how you want the sound to be used.

If we are in the battle scene and you want the characters to start talking, how clear will this sound? What are they doing while talking? Are they fighting with clanging and whistling Martian swords? Would they really be talking when doing this? Wouldn't it be better to wait until someone has fallen down and the other is standing over him? Better still, have all the talking done before the battlefield, in intimate settings and use a few metallic clashes after the scene to give an impression that the discussed battle has taken place.

Parties can also be difficult. On television or film, we can move from conversation to conversation around the room and focus in on what we want to hear. In radio there are two problems. One is that casts are small, so to create a party you have to ask all the cast to make party chat and laughter for a soundtrack. This is then looped behind the conversations. It's hard not to pick up on a background voice. In a loop we may hear this voice twice, saying the same thing twice – so the illusion is destroyed. It's also difficult for actors to gauge how to pitch their voices. Are they in the middle of a loud party shouting at each other? Are they at a quiet party talking softly to each other? Again, better to have a short burst of party sound to establish it – then move to a corridor, garden, or room away from the party where characters can talk in peace.

Over-Written Directions

It can be irritating for busy studio engineers to find a writer has been too specific and written a paragraph for them to digest and interpret. For example: 'A fish and chip shop on sea front. Sound of fryers, clattering plates and cutlery. Sound of about ten other customers at tables in the background chatting indistinctly. There is a road between the chip shop and the sea so some sound of cars and sound of the sea. Seagulls. There is a funfair nearby so some sound drifts in from that.'

This is too much. Really, 'a fish and chip shop on the sea front' is enough. Is someone going to rush out and get run over? Then mentioning the road is not important. Will we be going to the fair? If not, why mention it?

Write in what's needed, nothing more. Studio engineers are like good lighting cameramen on film. They know how to make a picture. It's up to you to specify what you need in the picture and leave them to it.

Also, remember that if you need the sound of an injured mallard trapped in mud, they'll find a way to create the scene. Even if it means a barefoot studio assistant stamping up and down in a bowl of papier mache flapping a sheet and blowing a duck birdcall whistle. Few challenges are unmet. Just be sure you need them and are specific.

Reading scripts and listening to plays will help give you an idea of how sound can be used adventurously, conveniently and concisely.

Controlling Backround Sound

If your characters are in a pub, it is usual at the start of the scene to put 'Pub sound loud', to give the audience a clear idea that we have moved to a pub. Then when characters start talking, write, 'Pub sound to background.' Or if you want the pub sound to remain loud because the characters, as part of the story, need to shout over it, then be sure to write this in.

Remember, sound can be used impressionistically as much as naturalistically. If we move from the pub to a jungle, It is worth writing, 'Burmese jungle sounds, night, for a moment', at the start of the scene, in order to let the new environment establish itself before the characters start talking.

At the end of a scene, you may want the sound to overlap. If you want to go from the pub to a bedroom scene for instance, it may be worth thinking about letting the sound carry through, to show the characters are still drunk. In that case write 'Pub sound fades under,' at the start of bedroom scene.

If you move from pub to bedroom cleanly it is helpful to put, 'Pub sound cuts' at the end of the scene, although this is usually assumed in the studio. If you want a very sharp cut between the pub and the jungle make that clear. At the end of the scene write, 'Pub sound plays for a moment then cuts sharply.'

It's better to write simply and precisely what you want than worry what the technical terms might be. If you want some pure sound before and after speech, be sure to write it in or the director may assume you want to go straight to dialogue or the next scene.

LOCATION, LOCATION

Radio plays don't always happen in studio. In contemporary plays a lot of energy can created by recording on location. Budgets usually mean a location recording will be picked for a play in Birmingham – not one in Brazil.

In location recordings, there's often a lot of standing around waiting for the plane to pass overhead, or tracking down the radio on the beach to get some peace to record. Some producers avoid location recording like the plague – it's time-consuming and risky. The advantages are that it energizes the actors. They are followed by a boom mike and don't have to worry about their position in relation to it as they do in studio. They can hear what sound they're acting against and adjust their voices accordingly.

Another advantage is a sense of space in exteriors. It simply sounds more believable that people are outside.

Using a location is a decision for a producer to make, and their headache to make it work. In most cases, the writer should assume their play will be recorded in a studio.

TECHNICAL TERMS

There are a few key technical terms. *Fade* and *Cut* for sound are fairly self-explanatory. *Fade Under* means a small overlap; we are in the pub talking about going to the jungle and next thing we know we are in the jungle... The use of the overlap is really to do with how connected the scenes are to each other emotionally or psychologically.

Similarly, if the characters are in the pub reminiscing about the time in the jungle, the link may be; *In background, jungle sound fades in over pub sound.* This direction could be placed to come in before the pub dialogue is quite finished, to indicate how vividly the characters remember their jungle experience.

SOUND AND SPEECH

A character can *Voice Over* in a radio script in just the way they can in film. They could speak over music, sound or other dialogue. For example:

BOSS   Mary, I don't know how many times I have to tell you it is not company policy to have fluffy animals on desks. It is against...(**CONTINUES UNDER VOICE OVER**)

MARY   (**VOICE OVER. INT.**) My boss has the longest, narrowest nose I've ever seen. Honestly you could open letters with it. If you could lift him up that is. Might need your friends to help, he must be at least eighteen stone.

BOSS   (**CONTINUING**)... health and safety. These things are a fire hazard and gather dust. Germs. They make the room look messy. What if everyone in the office had these? What are they, gonks? What if everyone had gonks? The place would look like a children's play pen, like a crèche. Mary are you listening to me?

MARY   (**ALOUD**) Yes, yes, no gonks, I get it.

The engineers will know to fade down the boss while moving the Mary actor close to the mike for an interior speech (INT). The sound will alter again when it's clear she's speaking aloud and not thinking.

Another useful sound direction is simply *D* for distortion, if someone's voice is coming through on a walkie-talkie for instance. Or simply write after the character name (ON WALKIE-TALKIE) and the engineers will know how to distort it.

If a character is in a gym, skipping, and this is established at the top of the scene, it is not really necessary to write (WHILE SKIPPING) in front of all their dialogue lines. If they stop skipping before speaking, that is an important stage direction to put in. To be fair to the actor, only a limited amount of skipping and talking at the same time might be feasible, although a character skipping while talking makes an interesting verbal texture.

How will the actor hold their script and skip at the same time? Possibly they can learn a few lines to say for a short skipping moment. Don't give the actor too much to say while skipping anyway; even a super fit boxer would probably stop if they have a lot to say. Experience and common sense will help you work out the right the balance between creating interesting verbal texture and humanitarian treatment of actors.

CHANGING VOICES

Sudden changes that will occur in a line of dialogue should be written for the actor, for example.

MARY I think I have a cold. (COUGHING) Or more likely, the flu.

BOSS How many days illness have you taken. (LAUGHING) How many different types of illness have you had?

MARY I can't help it. Since my divorce, I've been very run down (STARTING TO SOB). I seem to get every germ that's going round.

BOSS Mary, don't start crying. (GOING) The waterworks only work on me so many times.

Keep bearing in mind that actors can talk and walk. They can deliver their first line coming in and their last line as they leave. Of course, if your direction is an acting one, make sure you really want them to play the line this way before pinning them down. If an actor is coming in or leaving, it is a direction for the engineer too. They may have to follow the actor with a mike or direct them how far away they can be to be picked up clearly. If someone is coming in to a scene, it is usual to write (APPROACHING) in front of their dialogue.

The main points are to be specific about what exactly you need and not get bogged down in technical jargon. Place sound directions and speech directions where you want them and don't have too much, or too little.

Think of your use of sound as if you are composing a shooting script for a film. What are we hearing exactly? How long does it go on?

Don't forget, you're not alone. Give the basic, precise indications and let the experts make it come alive. And try not to annoy them with crowd scenes when you've got a cast of four.

BUILDING ATMOSPHERE

In the adaptation of Bruce Chatwin's story *A Coup*, I had to create a street riot in Africa. The dreaded crowd scene. I had also been asked to frame the adaptation with my own take on where the story was set, Benin, a country I knew well. The commissioners wanted the exciting Chatwin story set in context.

I put my own more meditative monologue into the past tense and Chatwin's into the present, as his story would be where the action happened. I voiced my monologue myself, to give it a flatter more reported tone than the richer, more varied tone of an actor's voice.

Good sound was essential to give the sense of a story welling up under the opening monologues. I wanted to build an atmosphere of confusion and hysteria – but knew I had a small cast. I decided with the director that the answer would be to layer the sound, repeat scenes to disorient the listener and give an idea of how confusion and danger was escalating.

The 'crowd' scenes were created by having the main action take place at a distance, outside the bar. Or having a small corner of the action in focus, such as the moment of Chatwin's arrest.

1 INT SMALL BAR A CITY WEST AFRICA

THIS VERSION OF SCENE DISTORTED AS IF IN A DREAM.
OUTSIDE THERE'S A RIOT. PEOPLE RUNNING AND
GUNFIRE. WHISTLES BLOWING, SCREAMS.

IN THE BAR THERE'S MUSIC ON TINNY CASSETTE, BOB
MARLEY, 'EXODUS'.

1 **WOMAN BARTENDER**
(**SCREAMING**) Get him out! Get that white scum out! You
want me killed? Mercenary! Murderer! Mercenary!

2 EXT. STREETS OUTSIDE THE BAR (CONINTUOUS FROM SC. ONE)

CHATWIN AND DOMINGO STEP OUT INTO A RUNNING
CREAMING CROWD. THEY START TO RUN.

1 **CHATWIN**
What did she call me? What did she say?
2 **DOMINGO**
Keep moving, down here.

SCENE CUTS SHARPLY

3 MONTAGE FOR MONOLOGUES

AN OUTDOOR SWIMMING POOL. SEA AT A DISTANCE.
FRENCH AFRICAN VOICES PASS MURMURING AND WALK
AWAY. PREDOMINANTLY THE SOUND OF THE POOL.

TOWARDS THE END OF THIS ANOTHER SOUND CUTS IN
INTERMITTENTLY, SOUND OF TAXI, OPEN WINDOWED
GOING THROUGH A BUSY AFRICAN MARKET STREET.
FLASHES OF THIS, LIKE RADIO INTERFERENCE.

1 **ANNIE**
I was alone in the pool at the Hotel de la Plage. It felt safe.
No one was going to run in and start shooting the place up.
Once though... (**PAUSE. SOUND FLASH**) Nine times in twelve
years they'd had a violent change of government here in
Benin, the bad old days. Then President Kerekou came,
nineteen seventy two, and he stayed, and he stayed.
(**PAUSE. SOUND FLASH**) He changed the name of the
country from Dahomey to the People's Republic of Benin. He
made friends with the Soviet block. Americans started calling Benin the Cuba of West Africa. (**SOUND FLASH**) Locals
called Kerekou the Chameleon, clever, shifting. Bullets and
bazookas ripped up the streets when his enemies and their
hired mercenaries tried to overthrow him. (**SOUND FLASH**)
I was safe in the pool at the Hotel de la Plage, a writer

researching a story. Once, another writer, the late Bruce Chatwin was passing by here, researching a story of a slave trader who made his fortune tearing flesh from this part of the continent... It wasn't safe then.

4 INT TAXI DRIVING THROUGH BUSY FRENCH WEST AFRICAN MARKET STREET

SOUND LOUD THEN TO BACKGROUND FOR VOICE OVER

1 CHATWIN
(VOICE OVER) I am with my friend Domingo, on our way to watch a football game, then we'll visit his uncles, who know stories about their ancestor the slave trader.

SOUND UP LOUD

2 DOMINGO
You see here and here, posters of our president on the building.

3 CHATWIN
That's Lenin.

4 DOMINGO
Yes, those are Lenin, over here's our president. You see his face, the marks, they tell us he is from the Somba people, from the north. Around here, around the presidential palace, this is the wealthy district, you know these flowers?

5 CHATWIN
Bougainvillaea.

6 DOMINGO
We call it something else... Ahead now see, the presidential palace itself?

7 CHATWIN
There's something going on.

8 DOMINGO
It's nothing. Traffic accident.

TAXI SLOWS, SOUND OF WOMEN APPROACHING AT A RUN, SCREAMING

9 DRIVER
It's the palace!

10 CHATWIN
It's not nothing.

11 DRIVER
It's war.

SOUND OF GUNFIRE NEARBY

TAXI SCREECHES AND TURNS.

12 **DOMINGO**

Drive down here, this way, to the left, to the left!

13 **DRIVER**

No good. Roadblock!

14 **DOMINGO**

Not this way! Stop, stop! There's fires ahead! Driver stop!

15 **DRIVER**

I can't! They're shooting. I can get home this way.

16 **DOMINGO**

Bruce, jump out and run. Now, do it! Go!

MOVING CAR DOOR OPENS

5 EXT STREETS (CONTINUOUS FROM ABOVE)

CAR DOOR SLAMS BEHIND CHATWIN AND DOMINGO AS THEY HIT THE GROUND STUMBLING, THEN RUNNING.

CHAOS DISTANT GUNFIRE. PEOPLE RUNNING, PANTING AND SCREAMING. WHISTLES BLOW.

1 **DOMINGO**

(RUNNING) Here, down here, in the bar!

6 INT SMALL BAR (AS SCENE 1) CONINUOUS FROM PREVIOUS

SCREAMS OUTSIDE. 'EXODUS' ON TINNY CASETTE.

1 **WOMAN BARTENDER**

(SCREAMING) Get him out! Get that white scum out! You want me killed? Mercenary! Murderer! Mercenary!

7 EXT. CITY SIDE STREETS (CONTINUOUS FROM PREVIOUS)

CHATWIN AND DOMINGO RUN IN TO SCREAMING RUNNING CROWD

1 **CHATWIN**

What did she call me? What did she say?

2 **DOMINGO**

Keep moving, down here.

A JEEP PULLS UP ACROSS THEIR PATH. CORPORAL AND ANOTHER SOLDIER JUMP OUT

CORPORAL

You, white, stop!

CHATWIN

(STOPS. PANTING) What's going on?

DOMINGO

He's not what you think.

CORPORAL

Shut up!

CHATWIN

Let go of me!

CORPORAL DRAGS CHATWIN TOWARD JEEP

CORPORAL

Move, for your own proper protection, move!

CHATWIN

Domingo, what is this? What have I done?

CORPORAL

(PUSHING CHATWIN INTO JEEP) Inside, get inside.

DOMINGO

(AT A DISTANCE) Bruce!

EXT JEEP DRIVES OFF HEADING PAST DOMINGO

(Excerpt from *A Coup* by Bruce Chatwin, adapted by Annie Caulfield)

Any crowd scenes were short intense and close in. The positioning of the sound also changes. At some moments we were close to Chatwin, at other moments outside the taxi or at a distance.

A sense of confusion can be created by changing focus of the sound. Just think about where the action is in a scene and set any other characters at a distance by writing OFF after their speech direction. This indicates they are at a distance, off mike.

Who is close and who is at a distance is, however, often a matter of common sense. Think about what the shot would be if this were a film. What's in close up? Chatwin being bundled into the jeep. What's in the background? Domingo left at the roadside.

WRITING FOR SPEECH

Writing for radio involves a lot of talking to yourself for a writer. How do words sound, rather than how they read on the page? Unless you are writing very formal characters, remember that in speech, people are more likely to say 'can't' than 'cannot' and 'don't' rather than 'do not'.

As you read aloud, think about the time your play is set. Is the language appropriate? Is it clear from the way a line is written that the character is not familiar with English? In a hurry? In a panic? In a subservient position to the person they're talking to?

Reading aloud will help you realize that you may have created an elegantly phrased tongue-twister. Too many similar sounds in a sentence will sound silly when spoken; sometimes sentences descend into simple sequences of hissing. The letter 'S' is a particularly tricky one when it occurs too often too close to the last S.

Think about the actor's need to breathe. If you try a sentence out and you run out of breath, don't assume that actors have some vastly extended lung capacity and will manage it. After all, they are playing an ordinary person with average lung capacity.

> I'd like to see more imaginative ideas about what characters are doing when they are speaking to one another. Listen to, and try to provide dialogue opportunities for what happens to our voices and our dialogue when we speak while we are: chopping vegetables, sewing, writing, mending something delicate, brushing hair; using scissors, eating, stroking an animal, typing, driving, painting, eating and drinking, putting on makeup, watching television...
>
> Marilyn Imrie, independent drama producer/director

WORDS AND VOICES

We hear the word 'beautiful' and think for a moment about the shape of the word, rather than agreeing or disagreeing with image of beauty presented to us. We think about what beautiful means as well as a visual image. We're guided in what the word means in a particular context by the tone of a reader's voice. The word could be uttered in awe, or disgusted sarcasm. Radio makes us listen more carefully for clues in the tone of voice.

Writing for radio, for words to be read aloud, we may find new qualities in mundane words. We might rediscover a word. We'd forgotten how much that word can sound chilling, joyful, or melancholy in an unexpected context.

As an exercise, write a list of the first ten words of one, then two, then three syllables that come into your head. Then write them into a line of dialogue with different contexts and see what interesting ways you can change the meaning of the word. How would the word sound slightly different each time when stressed in a different way? For instance, 'You've broken the best vase. Beautiful.' 'That vase is not so beautiful.' 'You think that vase is beautiful?' 'That vase you had, it was just beautiful.'

Once you've written each sentence, say them aloud to see how meaning changes emphasis, changes sound.

TELEPHONE, TAPES, TELEVISIONS AND TECHNOLOGY

One of the irritations to be found in radio scripts that was mentioned by several producers was the one-sided telephone call. It means the call has to be stylized, so the gaps for the unheard speaker are unnaturally short; or there are gaping silences. Why aren't you writing both sides of the call? If there is a reason, to create mystery perhaps, then fine. If you're worried about bringing in an extra actor to play a hotel receptionist or double glazing salesman that would be a bad reason – someone in the cast will have a voice flexible enough to play a few lines, slightly distorted, on a phone.

Where possible, think about having the other caller on a speaker phone. This is useful for scenes in cars. Your character can be travelling and talking at the same time. Are they making a mobile call while walking along? In this instance it might be difficult to hear both sides of the conversation. Although a character using a mobile is again useful for travelling and talking. The answer is probably to keep the conversation short – unless your play is about a man who has mysterious conversations on his mobile with an apparently monosyllabic person on the other end.

People talk to each other over the internet using web cams. Can you play with this?

Families are more likely to gather round a Wii game than a Sunday lunch table in many contemporary western households. Just because they're on the radio, they don't have to live as though they're in *Mrs Dale's Diary*. Thinking about all the technology we have in our daily lives can be an interesting way to change the texture of sound in a play.

We have machines in our lives that talk to us. Messages on answering machines can be extremely useful. Satellite navigation systems, email inboxes, burglar alarms... These machines provide a useful opportunity for a character to have a little chat aloud with themselves while apparently talking to a machine.

Often people don't hear each other coming these days because they're hooked up to ipods. This could be a useful way to create a startled beginning to a scene. Often people are in the same room and not hearing each other because one has headphones on. This could be something to play with.

I often wonder why people in radio plays seldom listen to the radio or watch television. One reason is that it can be messy to have too many voices in a scene that aren't relevant. But a familiar rhythmic noise such as a football commentary, the shipping forecast or weather forecast could be easily assimilated. Perhaps, if the person is watching late night poker, the shopping channel or a boxing match it tells us something about their character. The kind of person who keeps playing a computer game or keeps half an eye on the football while having a conversation can make for a realistic, stilted conversation.

Playing with the constant level of noise people have in their homes now could be an interesting way to create texture. As long as it becomes clear what the noise is and what it's doing in the scene, the chatter and beeping that surrounds us in the west could be a useful way to differentiate locations or to show us what kind of people our characters are.

EXERCISE IN SOUND

In a day school for adults wanting an introduction to radio writing, I had an interesting experience with this simple exercise. I ask people to shut their eyes and think of a sound that means something to them. This could be a way to conjure up a story, or to realize the variety of effects simple sounds can have.

One older man told us that his sound was absolute silence. He feels agitated if he's in a room and a hubbub of chat suddenly stops. Or if he's in a place where traffic can be heard outside and then someone shuts a double-glazed window to make the interior silent. This reminds him of being in London during the blitz, when bombs were falling and the most deadly moment was the strange vacuum of silence just before an explosion. A memory of sound, or lack of it, conjured up a whole other world in this man's story.

Think of sounds that mean something to you. What is the accompanying story? Perhaps this can be a springboard to the start of a play.

8 COMEDY

COMEDY IS DRAMA TOO

Although there has been comedy on speech radio for decades, possibly almost since radio began, writers tend to forget about it. If you look at the slots for comedy on radio, there is a huge scope to try out your dramatic talents. There is the half-hour sitcom and the fifteen-minute experimental comedy slot. There is also the comedy play.

Many contemporary play submissions are described as 'gloomy' or 'humourless' by producers. They all bemoan the scarcity of comedies in drama submissions. It may seem that the afternoon play and Friday play slots aren't the place for comedies. The simple fact is, there would be more comedies if more people wrote them.

If you're starting to write radio drama, you'll be ahead of the pack if you try for humour rather than angst.

FORGET THE SITUATION

A good comic play is character-based rather than situation-based. Avoid what sitcom writers call the 'Yellow Pages' school of writing. That is thinking – 'Somebody should do a comedy about air traffic controllers, traffic wardens, people working on the tube...'

For a start, the situations are seldom as hilarious as people imagine. Once in a while something mildly amusing happens. What is funny is people. And the right performers. There are dozens of workplace-based comedies but not all of them are *The Office*. Hundreds of cab drivers tell me, 'You could write a great comedy about this job.' I couldn't, until I was sure I'd grown brain smart enough to compete with Jack Rosenthal's London cabbie play *The Knowledge*. In this play the diverse eccentric characters provided story and laughter – the tribulations of learning to be a cabbie would otherwise have made a mildly diverting documentary. The situation is almost irrelevant; it's the ability to create and communicate the characters that makes a comedy work.

Where the situation matters is in 'the trap'. Tragic characters have choices; that's their undoing. Comic characters tend to have limited choices. They are related; they share a flat or a job; they are trying to learn something together; they live next door to each other; they are married; or they are in the Home Guard together. There are reasons why they can't just get up and leave. A situation where people are stuck together, be it in a family or workplace, recurs in comedy because it means people who don't like each other much, or have little in common, are forced up against each other. Within that, it sort of doesn't matter what they're doing, if they are funny enough.

THE CENTRAL LINE

In a drama, characters change and grow. Perhaps only fractionally, but they do tend to have had some experience at the end of a drama that changes them and their outlook. Often drama is about witnessing the process of change.

In comedy the main characters seldom grow or change. We also don't need their back story. Who knows or cares what Basil Fawlty's childhood was like. Comedy is very much about what's happening now. And we don't want characters to learn and grow. We want to rely on Basil Fawlty, David Brent, Larry David, Ed Reardon or Alan Partridge to remain the same fool they always were.

The characters like Harold Steptoe for instance, may be constantly striving to change. Harold Steptoe seemed to plan his escape in every episode but not only is he related to Albert Steptoe, but he's too weak to really go away. The fact that they are stuck is at the heart of comedy.

Alan Partridge veered from obscurity to success but never learnt how not to be obnoxious. Ed Reardon strives to be a successful writer and social charmer but he has to fail, or the series would be finished. Characters in comedy have an exterior trap, such as their job, their family or their poverty; but they invariably have an internal trap – their personality disorders.

If a character is funny and changes, they would probably be a good character for a single play. For a sitcom, the predictability of the central character is the heart of the joke. Who wants to hear Alan Partridge say, 'Oh dear, perhaps I was little pompous there, I apologize.' We want him to say something even more outlandishly pompous.

RADIO SITCOM

There are many successful radio sitcoms. Some, like *Absolute Power* and *Alan Partridge* transfer successfully to television. *Alan Partridge* had to change the format to be much broader and less restricted to jokes mocking radio for output. *Absolute Power* struggled to find a visual equivalent of its verbal wit.

Radio is not always a great place to try out your sitcom idea if you're hoping to move it to television. Radio and television work differently in terms of the type of comedy they do best. There is much more time for verbal banter on radio. Radio comedy is about wit. Think about how David Brent would have worked on radio. First of all we'd have not been able to witness the glorious horror of David Brent's famous dance, but we'd have missed the sickly grin and the smug expression that accompanied so many of his lines. Basil Fawlty's flailing limbs and Sybil's eye-rolling would have been no good on radio.

Although depending on performers with a good sense of timing and compelling vocal qualities, radio comedy is about the writing far more than the performance.

TRAVELLING WITH COMEDY

There is a lot of scope in radio comedy for the near monologue, such as *Ed Reardon's Week*. His loneliness and small obsessive life would be less interesting to watch than to hear about. Radio allows us better access to internal mental meanderings. When we hear about Ed Reardon's intentions, we understand what he feels about the petty things he's doing, rather than just witnessing the petty things.

Radio comedy can go anywhere. The excellent *Cabin Pressure*, about a small charter airline, would require a huge budget on television. On radio we say they're flying over the Sahara and are happy to accept that.

Radio comedy can go inside character's heads effectively. What people think they're doing and what they actually do, is often the heart of the joke on radio. The frequently cited radio classic *Hitch Hiker's Guide to the Galaxy* is a comedy that many people felt was a disappointment on television. All the scenes the words on radio conjured up couldn't be adequately created with a television budget. Things looked fake and silly rather than comically bizarre.

Similarly Andy Hamilton's *Old Harry's Game* would be an inevitable disappointment on television. *Old Harry's Game* is about the day-to-day administrative and demon management tribulations of Satan. Hamilton is able to conjure up all manner of fantastic grotesques and often quite violent situations, leaving the details to our imaginations. We're given occasionally striking images then left to picture the geography of hell for ourselves. The devil can go anywhere, transform himself into anything and torment people in outlandish ways on radio. Any famous dead person can turn up as a character. It's a rich, strange underworld but seen from the intimate point-of-view of an amoral but beleaguered Satan. It's a comedy that could only work so deftly on radio.

AUDIENCE SITCOM

Some radio sitcoms are recorded in front of a live audience. These tend to feature comedians who find it hard to get up to speed without an audience in front of them. They're used to judging their success by the audience reaction and find it uninspiring to work in a vacuum. Audience sitcom is for comedy with broader brush strokes, more set pieces and punchlines than something like *Old Harry's Game*.

In radio, as on television, writers tend to resist the live audience comedy. They feel it restricts them and simplifies the action. Sometimes, however it is hard to get the comic best out of performers without a live audience.

Sometimes a silence from a live audience forewarns of a line that seems great on paper but is lost in performance. And often, a broad brush stroke is still a funny one.

COMEDY STARS

It is not a good idea to say to a producer when you contact them, 'I see this as a vehicle for Graham Norton, Lenny Henry...' or whoever, unless you know the comedian and have discussed it with them. Preferably you will already have worked with them and know their strengths.

Many audience sitcoms are written by writers who always write for a particular comedian and have worked the comedy around them. If you feel you have a big central character, based on someone non-famous that you know, perhaps you could suggest a suitable comedian to or two to perform it when you submit your script. This could help give the producer an idea of the tone you have in mind. Far better to let your writing, whatever its style, speak for itself. If it needs a big performer and an audience, these will be found for quality writing.

PANEL GAMES AND QUIZZES

A successful panel game or quiz format is a sort of Holy Grail in comedy. These can run for series after series. Shows like *Quote Unquote, I'm Sorry I Haven't a Clue* and *Just a Minute* turn up again and again in the schedules. It's hard to think of a brilliant new format but always worth a try.

It is probably better to listen to a few existing panel shows to see how they work, then forget most of what you've learned. Apparently too many show formats submitted are very derivative. If you can write, 'The show will be a bit like...' in your proposal, then it's probably not original enough.

The competition element doesn't need to be serious. There may not be a competition at all. Perhaps the panellists have to make a judgement on something or give amusing advice. Panel shows are popular because they can be refreshed each week by different guests. They tend to disappear after one series where the format is too thin or too complicated.

IN THE NEXT ROUND...

Panel shows usually need some variety within the format. In the case of *Just a Minute*, the variety is provided by the fact that each person has a different topic that could go anywhere within the known universe. In the case of *Quote Unquote* there are sections where panellists are asked where quotations come from – these are usually from works of literature or famous people. Then there are sections where panellists bring in their own favourite quotations on different subjects, often sayings peculiar to their families. This way, the half hour changes direction a few times.

In, I'm *Sorry I haven't a Clue* there are all manner of bizarre rounds, sometimes included sometimes not, but at some stage in ancient history these were planned out by writers.

The round could simply be a diversion, sandwiched between the main format rounds as happens in *Quote Unquote*. It could mean several different tasks for the panellists as in *The Write Stuff*. In *The Write Stuff*, panellists could be asked about famous book openings and endings. They could be given a geographical location and asked to guess which book is set there. They could be given a physical description of a famous character in literature and asked who it is. They also have to produce a pastiche of a famous writer's style. It isn't a simple literary quiz.

Quizzes and panel shows often overlap. There are straightforward quizzes, such as *Round Britain Quiz* where getting the right answer to quite difficult questions is the point. Or there are quizzes that depend on the panellists being entertaining and able to go off at a tangent, such as *The News Quiz*.

There are quizzes on specialist subjects – food, business and geography themed quizzes come to mind. Writing down, 'What about a quiz on wildlife?' isn't a format. Think of different ways people could be asked questions. For experiments sake, let's think up our wildlife quiz. There would be a panel of animal experts, and perhaps a well-known animal show presenter such as Ben Fogle as the chair.

Round one: *Sounds and Signs.* Noises would be played in. What animal is it? Or some pawprints could be described. Or a type of animal dwelling described. Panellists would then have to identify the animal, adding in where appropriate any additional interesting information about why the animal makes that sound or constructs a dwelling that way.

Round two: *Animal Habits.* What animal does a particular peculiar thing? For instance, what animal sleeps twenty-three hours a day? Koala bears. Why do they do this?

Round three: *Animal Myths.* Is it true chameleons change colour to match their surroundings. That chimpanzees laugh? That elephants never forget?

As a non-animal expert myself I'm finding it hard to sustain this idea. Perhaps you need an expert friend to collaborate on your quiz idea. Perhaps the idea is too limited in scope. The other problem could be that when the quiz series gets beyond a certain number of episodes, all that's left to ask questions about is very rarefied information, so the general public would be alienated.

Wildlife, however, could be a good topic as it is something most people, even an urbanite like me, know something about and many people take a lively interest in the topic. *Gardeners' Question Time* has worked for years because there are enough people around Britain who take a keen interest in gardening and know a lot about it. A quiz about model railways will delight a small section of the population and leave too many of us baffled. If the quiz has to explain too much to be comprehensible to the majority, it will bore those genuinely interested in the topic.

Also, if I'm sitting at home and the idea of a wildlife quiz pops straight into my head, then there's probably something wrong with the idea. There may have been something similar in the past that might be revived. The format may have been discussed and abandoned. There are too many people trying to come up with new quiz formats on TV and radio for the obvious ideas to have been overlooked.

This doesn't mean a good format is impossible to devise, it will just take you some deft leaps of imagination.

PLAYING GAMES

Panel games that are based on old schoolroom games, such as *Would I Lie To You*, are most likely to have been pitched and tried out already. We all know the same childhood guessing games.

If you have a fresh idea and want to see how it would stretch to several thirty-minute shows, write it down as tightly as you can. Don't write things like, 'In this round the panel would simply improvize comic banter.' Even the best improvisers like a starting point. *The News Quiz* meanders all over the place but there is basic structure of questions and answers to fall back on.

If you know a famous comedian who has seen your format and wants to present it, then put their name on it. Otherwise you might suggest a couple of names as an ideal chair. Better to simply put 'light hearted panel show' as the subtitle on your proposal and allow the material to speak for itself.

BE PRACTICAL

Most of these shows are studio-based with a live audience; the budget goes on the guests. Far-fetched suggestions such as, 'Panellists are blindfolded and taken to different parts of Europe and then have to guess where they've been dropped, describing the scenery with humour...' are unlikely to succeed. Also if people are cold, hot or disorientated, they might not be very amusing.

Unless the panellists are professional comedians there are limits to how much they can improvize in entertaining asides. It's better to make sure the format provides enough for people to do if they're a weak panellist – questions to answer, prepared stories to tell, or structured strange things to do.

GAGS

If you can turn a great one-liner, it's worth sending in some samples to existing panel shows. If you listen at the end of the show and hear, 'Chairman's script by...' then it means there are gag writers on the show. Make sure your jokes are appropriate to the show but don't tailor them to a particular comedian too much. If you can write funny, write funny.

Keep them short. What these shows need is good one-liners not jokes with long set ups.

In topical comic panel shows like *The News Quiz* they are always looking for writers with a refreshing take on current events. Don't make the butt of your joke the reality TV star everyone regards as stupid, the footballer who's notoriously violent or the politician who's famed for their ugliness or crookedness – everyone will have done the joke before you.

For a topical show, sit down with the week's papers and find your own comic take on events. A good one-liner is a surprise. A lazy one tells the joke everyone sees coming – the economy's in such a bad state I wonder if they've put [dim reality TV star] in the treasury. Not only is this a limp joke, it's in the wrong order. It should read, if it has to be read – the economy's in such a bad state I think the treasury's being run by [dim reality TV star]. In one-liners, your funny word or name is the last one. As a vague rule remember, 'Whoops, I dropped my trousers!' is the ending for a joke; 'Whoops, my trousers are falling off!.' is not. Trousers is your funny word. He dropped what? His pen? A clanger? No – his trousers. Otherwise, within the sentence, you are giving away your punchline before the end.

If you send in your one-liners, perhaps a selection of fifteen, the show may take only two. They'll encourage you to send more and you'll get some small amount of money and a credit. Next time perhaps they'll take more. Next time they might ask you to become a regular writer on the show. Don't be disappointed if the initial joke sales ratio is small; it's still a foot in the door.

SKETCH SHOWS

Sketch shows are a very good way in to radio comedy. At the time of writing, *The Now Show* is the dominant topical sketch show on BBC Radio 4. As in the case of one-liners, try to avoid the obvious comparisons and references. Look at the papers, think of a few good sketches and send them in.

It's worth sending material in to any sketch shows where you enjoy the comedy. They may have their writers, but you may be steered to a show that needs writers. Address material to the producers not the performers.

SKETCH SHOW CONTENT

Radio sketches depend on wit and tend to be short. If your sketch is more than a side of A4 it's headed toward being a long sketch.

Try to give the sketch a shape. A sketch is like a tiny play. Each line needs to count and where it ends should be clear. Too many sketches set up a good frustrating situation and then end with something like 'Character goes raving mad, ranting around in style of Basil Fawlty.' This isn't an ending. Possibly it will work if you write the rant, in your own comic style.

As you can't swear much on radio, you don't have the cop out of ending a sketch on someone saying f... off; you have to be a bit smarter.

Songs and monologues are usually written by the performers themselves, or by their regular writers; sketches and one-liners are the way in.

If you want to write your own sketch show you will need to have developed a very distinctive style. If you write for a friend who is a great undiscovered comedian, the radio comedy producers need to be invited to see them perform. They will come; they need to find new talent. If you are a writer-performer, send in the sketches with suggestions of where you might be seen. Or make a good quality recording of your performance to send in with script.

If you have written a selection of sketches but don't perform, you might feel they were strong enough and sufficiently linked to merit a programme of their own, with performers being found for them. If you've written the radio equivalent of *Smack the Pony*, for instance, this could work out. Send in half a dozen sketches, explaining the theme of the show and how all the sketches are linked, offering to send in more to illustrate how easily you can keep creating enough for a series.

Usually sketch shows are performer-led. Ones that are not topical are based on characters the performers can do, such as in a series like *The Fast Show*. If you can create characters this strong on paper, the right performers will be found for you.

USEFUL STEPPING STONES

Once you're working on a show, you're meeting producers and performers. You can start suggesting your great sitcom idea or your panel game format.

Comedy is a very competitive environment. You may be the funniest writer on your college paper, but in the real world you'll probably have to work a lot harder to be the funniest. Having tough competition around you is a difficult but effective way to learn.

Writing sketches and one-liners is useful for all radio writing as it teaches economy with words. If you've only got one line, you soon learn to be very mean with your words. And to hear how one word in the wrong place can spoil a line.

TO BE AVOIDED

In comedy drama and sitcoms, it's felt there are far too many submissions that are spoof science fiction, spoof period drama and spoof chat shows. Versions of these formats have been brilliant, but attempts to be the latest great spoof seldom meet the mark.

In drama and sitcom it's also felt that too many submissions are workplace-based, set in the afterlife, at school reunions, the world of the media and in the past. Again, yours may be brilliant but you will have to defeat a slight heartsink from the producer when they see the familiar setting of your script.

Plays and comedies about writer's lives prompted many a groan until *Ed Reardon's Week* landed on someone's desk. But now there's a good writer's life comedy, why would producers want another? Perhaps yours has a twist so far away from the parsimonious English world of Ed Reardon the script will look fresh, but it would need to be a great twist.

Without resorting to the 'Yellow Pages' device of thinking up workplaces that haven't yet been a background to a comedy, you could think of an unusual setting and put your characters into it. Perhaps they write the catalogues of dinosaur bones for the natural History Museum. This suggests a geeky underground workplace in the style of the *IT Crowd*. Are your bone cataloguers characters that are recognizable to people who never knew such a job existed? Is their closed obsessive world familiar simply by being closed and obsessive? The characters, the lines and the forcing together of dysfunctional people should work in any environment. If you have a comedy about writers you feel would succeed if *Ed Reardon* wasn't ahead of you, perhaps the answer is to change what the characters do for a living.

Try not to compare your idea to another. 'An innovative science fiction comedy in the style of *Red Dwarf* in an accompanying letter is guaranteed to send producers to the next script in the pile.

Writing comedy, like writing drama, is all about asking yourself, 'Is this a story only I can tell? Is it based on a character only I can bring to life? If I was hit by a bus tomorrow, would they find it extremely difficult to get someone else to write episode two?'

9 WRITING FOR NON-FICTION RADIO

Most factual programmes are made by journalists; they are news or related to the news. That is an area of expertise for another book. However, there are areas where writers more used to writing fiction and using their imaginations can cross over into the area of non-fiction radio.

DRAMA DOCUMENTARY

Particularly for the afternoon play slot, the forty-five-minute drama documentary is very popular and undersubscribed. It's particularly suited to plays about everyday life. Your play could follow a fictional family facing homelessness, cut in with interviews with people from homeless charities, shelters and housing organizations. You might talk to families who have been made homeless and it's been disastrous – this would be a foreshadowing of what's to come for your family.

Whenever I have made a drama documentary, I've found ordinary people are far more useful than experts. Ordinary people speak in quirky ways, with passion, and don't trot out statistics. As an example, I was making a drama documentary about the poor in London, comparing and contrasting modern London with the London documented in Henry Mayhew's book *London Labour, London Poor*.

Mayhew wrote down what ordinary people said; I did the same. I found a few experts to interview but erased all these tapes – too dull. I copied Mayhew's work method – just wander around likely places with a tape recorder until you find someone to talk to you. Eventually I found great characters, like a teenager who'd set up a market stall selling produce used in African cooking. He was Turkish but he'd noticed his area of North London was now heavily populated with Somalis and Nigerians. As he talked, he painted a vivid picture of the area, he described his produce, he dealt with customers and gave me a lively criticism of official youth opportunity schemes. He told me far more about his part of Tottenham than any politician or social scientist.

Real people are touching to listen to, unguarded and distinctive. The first radio play I remember was about the flotilla rescuing troops from the beaches of Dunkirk. There was a fictional story about a boat going over and its captain, cut in with people's real memories of the day. Not always the obvious people. There were women who went to the port on the men's return with flasks of tea; there were people whose boats were too small or faulty and didn't go, leaving their owners with a lifelong regret.

How to Make a Documentary

To have a drama documentary play commissioned, you have to write in what you imagine will be gained from live interviews. What you'll gain will probably be much more.

If the play is commissioned, you can head out with your producer but recording equipment is now so small and easy to use, it's just as easy to go alone. In a one-to-one informal interview, your subject will relax more quickly. You can relate to them more personally.

It's better to have a very basic list of questions prepared, but think on your feet. If someone has a market stall and seems vibrantly articulate, don't stick to the questions about the poverty in their area – ask them to talk more about what they're selling. This way you have colourful descriptions of fruits and foodstuffs. Try to capture their interaction with customers.

Perhaps, if you're collecting reminiscences about the evacuation from Dunkirk, an interviewee mentions in passing that someone fell off the harbour wall. Abandon your next official question and find out about that incident. Anecdote makes good radio.

Interviews

As I mentioned, the technical side of recording interviews is quite simple as long as you remember to turn the microphone on, not to run out of batteries and not to bang the table, etc. Practise with your producer until you are at ease with the equipment.

Be sure the interviewee knows what the interview is for and that they sign a release form at the end, giving you permission to broadcast the interview. Sometimes people fear a trick, so its often a good idea to give them a sample of the type of question you want to ask, and explain why you'll be asking that, before you start.

Unless you happen upon an extrovert character to interview in their workplace, most people are shy of microphones. Find a quiet place to talk to them alone. Be prepared to use up a lot of tape just chatting until they get into their stride. If you are talking to someone about a sensitive subject they'll take a while to decide if they trust you.

Try not to fiddle about with the microphone and equipment too much, the important thing is to make the interviewee forget it's there. Don't wave the microphone around; try to rest your hand on something as much as possible. Be careful to follow the speaker with the microphone if they move their head some distance away, or their speech will be off-mike and indistinct.

Save your most awkward questions till last, until the person is used to you and the microphone. Don't ask multiple questions in one, such as, 'So some people say this is a poor area of London; has it always been poor or do you think it's deteriorated, with a lot more crime and vandalism?' If an interviewee can pick a question out of that to answer you'd be very lucky. Split up the questions and also, phrase them so that people don't give 'yes' or 'no' answers. So the multiple question above should break down to:

- 'What sort of area of London would you say this is?'
- 'How was this area when you were a child?'
- 'What changes have you noticed in the area?'
- 'What are the serious problems in the area?'

SOME INTERVIEW TECHNIQUES

Look at the interviewee, not the tape recorder, as much as possible. They may feel self-conscious and stop talking if they feel they've lost your interest. You should be listening carefully anyway, in case you find a new question to ask, inspired by their story.

Ask them to identify themselves on the tape at the start of the interview. Their name, what they do and any relevant information. For example: 'My name is Mary Pegwell, I was at the harbour when the boats came back from Dunkirk.' If you want to avoid using a narrator, the interviewees' own identifications will help introduce them smoothly. You should make a note on paper of the identification and where the interview is on the tape to save time and confusion later.

Leave space. Usually in a drama documentary, people's voices are cut in to the story and not the interviewer's questions. When you're sure they've finished speaking wait for a moment before asking a new question. Don't rush. This is not an abrasive cross-questioning of a crooked politician on a news programme with a minute to spare. Even if you are talking to someone quite accustomed to being interviewed, allow plenty of time for them to express their opinion. From a half-hour interview, you'll probably end up using a minute in the final documentary. The minute could come from the start of the interview, but is more likely to come towards the end, when the person has relaxed, got into their stride or been prompted to remember an anecdote they'd forgotten.

PUTTING THE DOCUMENTARY TOGETHER

There will be a long process where you go through the recordings with the producer and mark up the sections you think can be used. You then have to transcribe these into the script, so the engineer will know where the edit points are. Usually in drama documentaries, the writer goes in to the edit, but it's the engineer who will be able to hear you thumping the microphone all the way through; and this needs to be excluded and replaced.

In drama recordings, writers tend to be underfoot at an edit because the producer and engineer will have already ensured everything is professionally recorded. Until you are very experienced, you may find your interview recordings aren't as clear as you'd hoped.

By this stage you should have a rough idea where the real material slots in to the fictional script. Perhaps you'll need some music or a sound – the sea, a modern street, a siren – something to create punctuation between the script and the documentary.

Check that the rhythm is right; that we cut away from the drama at evenly spaced intervals. When collecting interviews and selecting those to include, be sure you have a wide selection of voices – young and old, male and female. Look for variety in the sort of interviews you use, some quiet, some ebullient, some sad, some amusing.

The drama documentary can be very time-consuming compared to writing a play, but it finds stories within stories, allows interesting asides and a far larger cast than you could afford if all the voices were actors.

PURELY FACTUAL PROGRAMMES

Although the magazine, documentary and news programmes have their own staff, there are places for freelance writers in radio. This may mean contributing a short section to an existing programme. Often you may need to hone skills, such as presenting and basic producing, to work in the non-fiction world. As with all radio programmes, with persistence, you'll find a door to open and work from there.

First of all, listen to the programmes. Is there a factual programme that interests you and seems to use written sections? Listen for the producer's name at the end of the programme and contact them directly. Their presenters may research and write their own material. A telephone call in the first instance may be nerve-racking but it saves wasting time.

Call the main BBC switchboard and ask for the producer by name and their programme by name. You should at least get an answering machine. I fell over a chair in my office while leaving a message for the producer of *From Our Own Correspondent*. I sounded like an accident-prone idiot – but he still employed me. They can only tell you to go away; no one can bite you down a telephone line.

At the end of the programme the announcer may say, 'This was an Accident Prone Production.' In this case, the *Writer's Handbook* or *Writers' and Artists' Yearbook* will tell you where to contact the company that makes the programmes.

SPECIALIZATION

If you have a specialist interest in physics, geology, sociology or fenland walks, for example, there may be a programme suitable for you. Send in a short pithy piece of writing on a fen walk you've done to the appropriate programme. This should be really short, no more than five hundred words. Write it to be spoken. Write it without jargon or overly complicated language. In your covering letter suggest that you are interested in working as a researcher and scriptwriter on the show. Or you would like a chance to write and present a short segment on your fenland. Be sure you are reasonably confident that you could talk about the fen without a script if you want to present. Perhaps you'd like to be taken on as a scriptwriter/trainee producer on the programme. Tell them this and you never know. There may be something in your expertise and the stylish way you write about the subject that will persuade them to give you a chance.

WRITING STYLE

Your five hundred words on the fenland walk should begin enthusiastically and with a startling fact. Radio doesn't do statistics and description well. It is a medium for anecdote and little chunks of fact. For example, don't say, 'This fen is probably two miles deep. Scientists have been measuring it with sonar. It is possible however to walk around the two kilometre path on the northern shore.'

This needs a lot of bringing to life. This might be better: 'Fall in this fen, and you could sink for two miles. Sonar recordings suggest that's the deepest the black murky mud gets here. So whatever you do, pay attention to the signs telling you to keep out and walk along the path.'

Then move quickly to the walk on the path. What plants and birds do you see? Keep us with you on the walk in the present tense. Is there a myth about a monster in the fen? Were witches drowned in it? Did a herd of cattle once charge in and disappear? Lively pieces of information will draw the listener in.

This writing sample is not the place to show off too much scientific knowledge. You need to show that you understand how to communicate popular science. If you have a PhD in Fens, put that in your covering letter. What the producers of this type of show are looking for is experts who can come out of their laboratories and explain things, enthuse the uninformed and entertain the knowledgeable.

YOUR PASSION

As you may have gathered, I know nothing about fenlands. I can't imagine anything worse than studying fens. There would be no point in me contacting a science or nature programme looking for work on their popular fen walk series. Where my passion lies is travel and I do some radio work as a result of sending in written pieces and ideas for programmes where the country and topic are very well known to me.

For example, I wrote three paragraphs that I hoped were entertaining and informative about the film festival in Burkina Faso. I explained how I would go about making a programme on the festival, who I would interview and what I would investigate. Because I already knew Burkina Faso, and the film festival, the proposal convinced a producer to send me off to make the programme.

This wasn't completely out of the blue. I had published travel books and worked for *From Our Own Correspondent*, but it was my first official 'Written and presented by...' credit. I knew my subject and had spent ages writing the pitch – this convinced more than my stammering attempts in a rehearsal presentation could.

Everyone in broadcasting knows that everyone has to start somewhere. If you work on your pitch, know your stuff, you might be given a chance.

Although I Fell Over...

Although I fell over during my initial phone call to *From Our Own Correspondent*, I did get the producer to read my piece and have worked for them several times since. This a programme well suited to the writer. It focuses on what lies behind the news and gives dimension to the news.

I was fortunate that I'd been travelling in and writing about French West Africa. Most BBC journalists were in Iraq or Afghanistan. They were where the action was. I was where some small fragment of unreported action was.

The programme aims to shed light on the whole world, so freelance writers who've been somewhere strange or witnessed something unusual in a familiar foreign location are in with a chance. *From Our Own Correspondent* pieces are eight hundred words long, exactly. They have the shape of a short story rather than a news item. They begin in a very active way, often using a lot of direct speech. The writing has to paint a picture of the people who are talking, the place they are and make it clear what is happening.

You will read the piece on air yourself, so be sure that it's not full of words you can't pronounce. When you practise it, take your time. Most untrained people speak far more quickly than they imagine.

The piece doesn't have to be serious. It's very easy for correspondents to find doom and gloom all over the world, so a story that is a little uplifting or entertaining gives a freelancer a good chance to find a slot.

Trying to get a slot on *From Our Own Correspondent* is very competitive. The fee is very small, so it is the prestige of the programme that draws people to write for it. Also, journalists like a chance to write up some anecdote, some quirky behind-the-scenes moment they've witnessed, rather than always looking for headlines.

The piece below is an opening for a very light-hearted piece I wrote and recorded after a trip to a surprisingly dull Spanish festival. The producer liked the humour and felt it provided an insight into Spanish rural life that undercut the holiday brochure image. It's an example of the very active prose required for radio.

Posters are going up around the small northern Andalucian town of Huescar. Reading them, with my tourist Spanish, I gather a fiesta is coming and it will be 'More exciting than ever! With free beer!'

A shopkeeper I question is vague about the fiesta: 'Oh, people come from miles around, it takes over the town park for a week, everyone comes.'

'Everyone comes to do what?' I ask.

'Oh, they bring sheep and drink beer.' The shopkeeper is too busy for my questions and I have run out of Spanish. I expect there is a lot more to the fiesta than this.

In the park, wooden pens are being constructed. I see new tractors being arranged fetchingly in marquees - I realize that this is the local agricultural show.

Still, I'm in Andalucia, there's bound to be more colour to the proceedings than I'd find in Ambridge. Perhaps the sheep that arrive to fill the pens will be fierce, the locals might fight them with capes....

On the opening day, I find sheep being looked over by rosette-wielding judges, but they seem to expect nothing more from the animals than sufficient sheepliness. Although, the beer is free, if you can feign enough interest in buying a new tractor.

I see a man handing out programmes; now I'll find where the excitement really is... But there are very few events listed that don't have 'sheep' in the title.

I understand that for the local farmers this event is an important place to meet and do business; sheep matter in these dry scrubby hills. But why promise excitement?

Then I spot a highlight in the programme. A demonstration of new methods for artificial insemination of a sheep. Not something I would normally go out of my way to see, but I'm getting desperate.'

(Excerpt from *From Our Own Correspondent* contribution by Annie Caulfield)

IT'S ALL WRITING

Changing direction, posing questions, introducing new characters – all the techniques that apply to writing radio drama also apply to writing radio prose.

If you feel your writing and ideas are suited to documentary writing, there are suggested ways in on the invaluable BBC website. To really show what you can do, it might be worth making a fifteen-minute piece on your own. Perhaps put this on the internet and refer potential employers to it. A basic microphone and digital recorder won't cost you a fortune. Ask in a specialist shop what would be best for your purposes. They should be able to advise on a good simple computer program to use for editing, that won't cost you a fortune. Students on media courses have access to good editing equipment for free; find such a student, and make them your friend. Editing your programme would be good practice for them.

You could go to a professional sound studio for the edit, but try to make this spec programme for nothing. Wait till you've had some reactions before making a large financial outlay.

MAKING YOUR PROGRAMME

Script your documentary to have a shape, like a story. What have you set out to find out at the start? What do you want to show people? Are you surprised in the end? Are you more enthusiastic about the subject than when you started?

If you are going to cut in interviews, make sure they are lively, have variety and build the story. You may be a natural at talking off the top of your head into a microphone. If not, write down what you need to say, using language as fresh and cliché free as possible. If you are just going to talk, jot down the main points you have to make in the section to keep the story moving and get your information across.

If you have no budget, you may have to pick something small. Do you have a friend with a weird hobby? Is there a bizarre local event? Do you have a remarkable neighbour? I have a neighbour, for instance, who lives without electricity, gas or an inside toilet, by choice. He's eighty years old, chatty, happily self-contained, full of reminiscences and also drives an enormous vintage sports car. I would love to make a little portrait programme on him.

If you want to write and produce documentaries, you'll probably get to wildly adventurous locations, after you've kept listeners fascinated for fifteen minutes with the man next door, your weird friend or your village dog pageant.

10 ADAPTATIONS, ABRIDGEMENTS AND BIOGRAPHIES

ADAPTATIONS

A large percentage of the BBC drama output is adaptations. These can be novels but are sometimes poems, diaries or historical works with a strong storyline.

Unfortunately, the slots for adaptations, particularly of the high profile classic serials, do tend to be taken by more experienced writers. However, you may have a family diary or history, of broad general interest, that you feel uniquely qualified to adapt. Is this an unpublished diary of a woman who did something remarkable? Is it a history of a nudist colony you were brought up in? Is it an unpublished novel by a famous dancer that you knew? Is it a short story by a famous author that's about something you've been through in real life? A personal passion or connection can count for more than writing experience. In this instance, if you are new to radio drama, it is worth adapting at least a quarter of the book to send in with the manuscript to show your dramatic skills are up to the task.

If you are quite an experienced writer, it's still a good selling point to make it clear that you have a special connection with the work you want to adapt. Looking for connections can strengthen an adaptation. It may be that the adaptation will only form the core of a modern drama that you weave around it. Have you found a book that tells the story of a dangerous sea crossing in the eighteenth century? Have you made that crossing lately? Have you found a little-known eighteenth-century novel about an adopted child with experiences that echo your own upbringing? Perhaps juxtaposing your story and the book could make a powerful drama.

In general it is better to begin writing radio drama showing you have your own voice. Adaptations do involve a lot of craft. It is worth listening to them and looking at the scripts to get an idea of different ways radio can be used.

NARRATIVE VOICE

Preferences vary from writer to writer and producer to producer about how much narration to use. Currently, the feeling is that people want a flavour of the original prose, so a narration provides this. Too much narration can spoil the sense of a story unfolding *now*; too little can leave the listener a bit lost. An energetic, active narrator, such as the Charles Dickens in Mike Walker's script of *David Copperfield*, excerpted on page 101, gives a sense that there will be signposts along the way and that the narrator will keep involving the listener in the story.

Where possible, the narrator should speak in the present tense. Drama is about what is happening at this moment and what is going to happen next. It may be that what we want to know is what has happened. Who killed the mayor? But our investigation should be conducted in the present, moving forward through the clues, even though they go back to the past.

Look at the openings of some of your favourite classics. How can that perfectly-phrased opening paragraph be made active rather than reflective? Try changing the opening paragraph to the present tense while keeping the flavour of the original. This may all sound very blasphemous but novels are often about people's reactions to events, people's thoughts on what has happened. In a drama we need to *witness* what has happened. In drama we need the sense of being in at the start of a story rather than being given a wise overview.

COMPLAINTS

If you interfere with someone's favourite novel, it may be that nothing you do will please them. I was recently very disappointed with the film version of *No Country for Old Men*. I thought whole layers of meaning had been stripped out of Cormac McCarthy's novel. They'd even downgraded the novel's central character, the sheriff, to a much less important role Then I realized that the meaningful sections were in the sheriff's diary. The filmmakers had dropped him in favour of characters who were doing more and thinking less. They had stripped the story down to the film, the parts where things are happening. It was perfectly satisfying to people who hadn't read the book. It did keep the atmosphere of Cormac McCarthy's world. It made some, I expect, pick up the next Cormac McCarthy book they saw and read it. A good adaptation has to ignore the sensibilities of the knowing fan, and to communicate with those who haven't read the book yet.

Complaints that an adaptation is 'lifeless' suggest the dramatist has failed. If the complaints are that the adaptation is 'disrespectful' or has ignored whole sections of the book, then it might be a good drama.

ADAPTATION OF DAVID COPPERFIELD

In Mike Walker's adaptation of *David Copperfield*, Dickens, the narrator, is talking to us in the present tense. As if he is making up the story at that moment. Liberties are taken from the start in the interests of drama.

FADE UP

NEUTRAL BACKGROUND

DICKENS:

This is a story about a boy named Daisy – or Trotwood or Doadie or Davey or David Copperfield or D. C. And as we all know, stories are the only things in this world that are really true because they never try to tell the truth.

HE PAUSES –

Well, that sounds like mirror talk to me – but then...

HE GETS UP, CROSSES THE ROOM, TAPS A MIRROR

What do we see in the mirror? The truth or it's opposite? And what does the mirror see in us?

WE FADE UP COTTAGE INT.

A DOOR OPENS AND BETSEY ENTERS THE COTTAGE UNDER

A visit, shall we say, of an elderly lady - Miss Betsey Trotwood - to a young woman, a very young woman who is the widow of Miss Trotwood's nephew, a certain David Copperfield. Are you with me?

SHE'S CROSSED THE SITTING ROOM – THE CLOCK STRIKES TWO. SHE OPENS THE KITCHEN DOOR – CLARA IS HUMMING AS SHE WORKS

BETSEY:

(LOUD) You do not know me!

CLARA CRIES OUT IN SHOCK AND DROPS A PAN

But you have heard of me?

CLARA:

Ma'am?

BETSEY:

Betsey Trotwood.

PAUSE

Your late husband's Aunt?

CLARA:

(UNDERSTANDING) Oh. (WAILS) Ohhhhh

BETSEY:

Now... stop, girl.

CLARA SNUFFLES

Take your cap off – let me see you. You are a child, aren't you? So young to marry, too young to be a widow and as for carrying a child... God help us...

CLARA WAILS

When's she due, the little girl?

CLARA:

Why... I...

BETSEY:

Why Rookery?

CLARA:

Rookery?

BETSEY:

The cottage. Why is it called the Rookery?

CLARA:

My dearest.... husband named it. He liked to think of the rooks settling on the roof.

BETSEY:

Do they?

CLARA:

No... they don't.

BETSEY:

Better have called it Cookery. That would have been practical. Not that he ever had a practical thought. Well, we may hope his daughter will be brighter. What do you call your girl?

CLARA:

It might not be a girl, I hope for a...

CLARA CRIES OUT IN PAIN

BETSEY:

The servant, what do you call...

CLARA:

Peggotty.

BETSEY:

Is that a name? (**CALLS**) Peggotty, your mistress needs a cup of tea. Now. She is overcome.

THE DOOR OPENS AT ONCE – CLARA CRIES AGAIN

Forget the tea, call the doctor.

THE DOOR CLOSES

Come along, sit down, girl. Do you have money?

CLARA:

Mr Copperfield left...

BETSEY:

How much?

CLARA:

A hundred and fifty a year.

BETSEY:

That, at least, is something. Now... sit... sit, child... and breathe. Yes, breathe. I'm sure the doctor will agree with me: breath whilst we wait for my... great niece...to arrive.

CLARA:

But I do think...

BETSEY:

I have a presentment. A girl child and you will call her Betsey Trotwood Copperfield and we shall make sure, you and I, that she is never trifled with, that her life is not... full of false confidences and lies and affections that...

SHE CUTS HERSELF OFF

Betsey Trotwood Copperfield. You wait and see, my dear girl, all will .... I believe that is the doctor.

THE DOOR OPENS

Doctor, attend your patient!

CLARA CRIES OUT – BETSEY CLAPS HER HANDS
Hurry, my great niece will not be kept waiting!

AS CLARA WAILS WE MIX TO:

SITTING ROOM LATER – THE CLOCK STRIKES SIX

A PAUSE – A CRY OFF, A BABY'S WAIL

DOCTOR:

(**VO**) It's a boy.

BETSEY:

(**CALLS UP**) Nonsense – look again, you fool.

DOCTOR:

(**VO**) It's a boy!

BETSEY:

Well.... Well ....whatever use is a boy!

THERE'S A PAUSE AS SHE CROSSES THE ROOM, OPENS THE FRONT DOOR

A boy!!!

SLAMS IT.

Dickens, the narrator, invites us to begin listening to a very familiar story with a new thought. The story then begins and the action is thick and fast. There are no characters we don't need to hear from and no moving from place to place to create energy. The energy is all in the dialogue as it tells us what's happening and the changes of tone move from humour, to pain, to rage.

> Be irreverent; don't stop at every station in the existing plot; experiment with what happens if you move the chronology of events to clarify the story; consider creating a character that the author didn't create, if in doing so an element of the plot becomes clearer for the audience. If it is a first person narrative, remember that their interpretation is only partial; consider going where the narrator can't go, and see what happens there without them, e.g. what happens in Italy between Little Emily and Steerforth in *David Copperfield*; what happens to the housekeeper in *The Remains of the Day* when she leaves the big house and the butler; what happened to Mr Rochester's wife to make her mad? ... What do Bridget Jones's friends/parents and lovers get up to when they are not with her?
>
> Marilyn Imrie, independent radio producer

TAKING LIBERTIES

Adaptation is a place for a writer's inventiveness with drama to blossom. Are there ways to turn internal thoughts into dialogue? Are there ways that an extended description of a journey can be turned into a rendition of a journey? Decisions have to be made with long books as to what is the heart of the story. Dialogue that looks convincing on the page may be too wordy or too consistently monosyllabic for radio drama. There may be too many subtexts to cram into a few hours playing time. If a novel is told from several points of view, will all of them be confusing in a drama? Do you need to pick just one? Characters may have to be invented to create dramatic exchanges. Characters who feature strongly in the book may have to be dropped back as they distract from the main story and only express a theme in the novel. Language may have to be altered if it is too archaic or arcane, leaving an impression of how the people in the book speak rather than replicating it.

Some adapters suggest reading the book, then writing a rough outline of the story as you remember it. Use this outline to construct the play's first draft and only then go back to the book to find the dialogue you can use, the good scenes you've forgotten and the sub-texts and themes you can begin to work into the play.

Here is some advice from John Taylor, creative director of Fiction Factory Productions:

- Distil the number of characters down to the bare minimum.
- Seek clarity of character and storytelling throughout.
- Make all encounters significant.
- Ensure each scene has its own tension.

When I interviewed experienced dramatist Sarah Daniels, she shared these thoughts on adaptation: 'What would I advise someone adapting a book? To be as faithful to the intention and spirit of the original author as possible. To know that this is not your voice but theirs and at the same time give it everything you've got as though it were your own.'

It could be a useful exercise to think of a book you love and make some notes on dramatizing it. This may help you to experiment with technique rather than worrying about telling your story and creating characters. Play around with several approaches to dramatizing the book, trying different ways to make us feel as though we are in the middle of the story rather than reviewing events reflectively with the prose writer.

ABRIDGEMENT

There are many story slots on radio, such as *Book at Bedtime* and *Book of the Week*. Here there are small budgets and the producer usually abridges a book themselves. These are faithful readings of the text, sometimes overseen by the author themselves if they are living. Abridgements are usually faithful renderings of the sections of text selected.

Some abridgements are broken up with dramatized sections; this often occurs on *Woman's Hour*, but the dialogue will be drawn from the book. A dramatist may be involved in these 'dramatized abridgements' but the slot tends to go to experienced writers as distilling a book down takes some experience.

BIOGRAPHY

A biography of, for example, a famous singer, could be an interesting afternoon play. You may have something in your own experience that enables you to grasp aspects of the singer's life in ways others couldn't. You may have spotted a moment in their lives that would provide a great drama – the car crash that blinded them, the love affair that destroyed them.

The play will not be a cradle-to-grave rendition of a life. The play should centre around a defining moment. The rest of the life can provide colour around the drama that you are writing.

A biography play shouldn't be an adaptation of a biography. It's better to draw from several sources, particularly your own imagination. If you couldn't have found the information anywhere but in the authorized biography, you may need to credit the biographer, gain their permission and give them some royalties. These are things to discuss with the producer. In the first instance, if you discovered that Singer A had an extraordinary friendship with Philosopher B and want to make a play from their relationship and what you imagine they said to each other, start writing it and then worry about permission.

> The historian, essentially, wants more documents than he can really use; the dramatist only wants more liberties than he can really take.
>
> Henry James, *The Aspern Papers, 1909*

If you are writing about someone centuries dead, you can take a lot more liberty than if they died in 1950. On the other hand if your story is a clear fantasy, such as, for example, Jimi Hendrix secretly went on a space mission, then no one can object to your play on grounds that it's inaccurate – it's clearly fiction. Where your play claims to be biographical and accurate, the public service aspect of BBC broadcasting may require permission from living family members. If your subject is alive, you will need their permission to write about them.

YOUR VERSION OF A PERSON

If you didn't know the famous person you've chosen to write a play about, then you have to do some detective work on their character. Accumulate evidence on how they talked, interacted and behaved when alone. Of course there will be conversations, encounters and thoughts that you imagine.

Your rendition can't be a photograph, but it should be a decent sketch, or possibly a cartoon rendition of the person. If you are going to take your picture of them very far away from the known facts, why pick that person? Why not just invent someone similar?

WHAT DRAWS YOU TO THE BIOGRAPHY?

A biography play falls in between fact and fiction, adaptation and original drama. If you have a burning desire to write about someone, then that's probably a good place to start writing radio drama and worry about the technicalities later.

If you want to write about Jimi Hendrix because you think people would like to hear a play about him, you aren't proving yet why it should be you who writes the play. Is there something about him other than the fame that you want to explore?

I was asked to write a play about Irish writer Flann O'Brien. What I found fascinating about him wasn't his prodigious drinking, or that most of his real fame was posthumous. It was the fact that he took on responsibility for a vast extended family and held down a job at the civil service. Behind his life as a flamboyant character in the pubs of Dublin, there was this diligent dutiful man. He was trapped in drudgery but also welcomed the drudgery as it kept him fixed in reality and a semblance of respectability.

It is usually the unexpected detail, the unlikely habit, or fear, or friendship that makes a good central core for a biography play.

A famous person's life may be more exciting than most, but what happened to them that you and the audience can strongly identify with? Where's the ordinary note in their noisy existence. What makes the story of their particular strange life universal?

11 SOAPS

Currently there aren't many radio soaps on air, so this chapter is a little shorter than it might have been five years ago. Popular with millions, the world service medical soap, *Westway* has been dropped in favour of rolling news. There is *The Archers* on Radio 4, of course. This runs and runs, with many thousands of loyal listeners. Like it or loathe it, *The Archers* is the first radio drama many people get to know; it's how people all over the world come to understand the idiom.

Channel 4 radio and online stations will probably develop more soaps to attract and hold radio audiences. Soaps come and go on BBC stations, so they may be back. Some people might be happy to hear of the current demise of radio soaps. They aren't the most challenging form of drama. But they do keep an audience and keep people in work.

The rural setting of *The Archers* that sometimes seems old-fashioned is actually quite topical at the moment, as people struggle to eat organic and want to know where their food comes from. The seasonal concerns and struggles to keep solvent in the lives of farmers inform listeners about things they're very interested in. Similarly, *Westway* went out to many places where the medical information was sparse or ill-understood. The programme-makers would glow with pride to get an email from the World Health Organization congratulating them on their long running Aids storyline. Or asking that they include a storyline about the correct treatment for dehydration in the under-fives to help mothers in hot countries – I don't remember how they created a case of a dehydrated child in rainy west London but they managed it.

Westway also began as an aid to people learning colloquial English, there was an accompanying programme where phrases such as, 'put my back out' and 'kick the bucket' were discussed and explained. This programme was dropped as it had few listeners and it became clear everyone listened to the soap because they loved the story and the characters, never mind the English lesson.

SOAP WRITING

Soap characters are like sitcom characters. The audience expect them to react in predictable ways. If a character is a Lothario, it's disappointing when he settles down devotedly with a wife. It's sort of the end of his story. If a character is a domineering battleaxe, audiences want to see her defeated. But also miss her if she's crushed into keeping quiet. In soaps, character is story. Characters might step out of character for a while when events overwhelm them, but a silent cheer goes up when they return to behaving badly, saying terrible things or scaring the neighbours.

Well-written soap opera episodes have characters behaving as we would expect but in new and subtle ways. The characters react and speak as we'd hope, but more so. In a good sitcom like Larry David's *Curb Your Enthusiasm*, we are filled with glee as Larry walks into a situation where we know he'll mess up, where we know he'll say the appallingly cringe-making wrong thing. Soap operas are the same. We want the bad guy to be bad, the silly guy to be silly – the surprise is in *how* they do it this time. The sense of, 'I wonder what's going to happen next?' is really, 'I wonder how what I know is going to happen, will happen next?'

SOAP WORLDS

Soap operas are an odd form of drama for radio. They have a naturalism and tendency for people to say what they mean that goes against what writers attempt to do in good original drama.

As so much of what happens in soaps is emotional, radio struggles to find words for those looks of horror, shame and loathing that abound in TV soaps. Writers often cringe when they listen to radio soaps but, like everyone else, if the story is gripping they'll forget the 'tell all' dialogue and get to the cliffhanger at the end wondering if they'll be near a radio for the next episode. Just to check that it all turns out as they'd predicted of course.

> There is scarcely any less bother in the running of a family than in that of an entire state. And domestic business is no less importunate for being less important.
>
> Montaigne, *Essais*, 1580

Soaps centre around family life and heightened domestic problems. They present worlds that seem familiar – friends, neighbours, dysfunctional sibling relationships. People watch the emotional traumas and often feel, 'Good, not just me then.'

Soaps also present communities as we would like them to be. People in the community are committing slander, murder, adultery and crimes against hairdressing, but they are a community. People talk to their neighbours, help the man in the shop, form friendships with pub landlords. In the west, real life is much more dissociated than this. People in communities are increasingly not connected or relating to each other. Soaps thrive in the western world because they present a nirvana of belonging.

JOBS ON SOAPS

The Archers has a small, established team of writers, although they do take on new writers every so often, once they feel the writer is suited to the programme. Soap teams tend to stick together for a long time as so much of the writing depends on knowing the characters well.

In general, soap writers need to have some experience because they have to work very fast. They can have a week to write a draft, then a matter of days to incorporate any rewrites. A great deal of information has to be conveyed in an episode and a long-established programme style understood and maintained.

The good thing about writing soaps, apart from a regular income, is a discipline imposed on your writing life. There's no waiting for inspiration; the job has to be done in the time allocated, with the restrictions imposed on you. *The Archers* is less than fifteen minutes long, as was the now-departed *Westway*. To get in story, humour and atmosphere in such short spaces of time really hones writing economy. Characters who aren't in episodes for a while have to be referred to – are they on holiday, away on a course, or just on their way to the shops. Otherwise people start to wonder, 'Mrs Archer, where's your son, what have you done with him?' An episode quickly fills up with things that need to be said, leaving little room to manoeuvre.

There is also, for the solitary writer, a camaraderie in the soap team script meetings. Most soaps have a six-monthly meeting to do long-term story planning and then a monthly meeting to plan storylines coming up. When the writers get on, these are fun; when they don't, it can be a battleground. Either way, it makes a pleasant change from struggling alone with your great masterpiece.

The challenge of making a good cliffhanger for your episode is an entertaining thing to write. Finding new twists on the infidelities, betrayals, accidents, financial traumas and failures that are the stuff of soap operas is more challenging and involving than many writers might imagine. Once you start writing on a soap, those characters are yours and you'll find yourself shouting in script meetings, fighting to make their lives dramatically exciting and deeply moving.

DIGITAL AND ONLINE SOAPS

The digital station BBC Asian Network has a soap called *Silver Street*. This is worth finding and listening to as it has a more flexible writing team and is keen to hear from new voices. If you have an original script that shows you are familiar with the type of people and situations that crop up in *Silver Street*, this would be a better way to approach them than writing an imaginary episode on spec. *Silver Street* is modern, quite urban, multicultural but full of familiar community-based soap stories. If you recognize the world of *Silver Street*, empathize with the characters and enjoy the stories, it could be a way in to soap writing. Although the budget for writers' fees is not immense, it's a good quality place to start.

If they like your writing and they have spaces for writers coming up, all soaps have a scheme to put you on, so you understand how the programme works and how to write to their template.

The online station Channel 4 Radio is beginning an online soap in 2009, a spin-off from *Hollyoaks* called *Runners*. Start watching *Hollyoaks* now to see the programme's world. Once it is up and running, *Runners* could be a way in to soap writing.

Another online soap is *Spinning Jenny*. This is full of lively stories set in Manchester. Listen and decide if you have something to offer. Then contact the producers to see if they'd be interested in reading your material. Independent online soaps will probably have no money for you but could give you a chance to learn and get a credit.

Online soaps are proliferating and provide a good entry into the world of soap writing. Keep checking the web for new ones – just Google 'online soap' – and decide if they appeal to you. Writing soaps is hard work so if you feel cynical about them and can't find something in the particular soap that appeals, you're probably wasting your time starting down this writing route. Otherwise, keep contacting any you find because their needs change and a rejection can always contain good advice about the next door to knock on.

SOAP ROUND-UP

The advantages in all soap writing are learning to have a dexterity in your writing, getting into the habit of writing on a regular basis and learning how to bring your imagination to play even in a very limited framework. Soaps are a great place to learn how to tell a story in dialogue, using the fewest lines possible.

12 PRACTICALITIES

SCRIPT LAYOUT

No need to worry about this - there is a free, user-friendly radio drama template to download on the website bbcwritersroom.com. If you aren't technologically minded, here are a few basic rules. In radio drama, the character names go on the left hand side of the page, with a clear space to the right of the name before the character's speech talks:

ANNIE   Make sure the space is the same all the way down the page so the script doesn't look jumbled. So measure it from the character with the longest name. Or abbreviate long names.

The layout is like this because radio scripts are read, not memorized. It is the easiest way for actors to see the lines. Character names should be in capitals, dialogue in lower case. Try to put each sound effect on a separate line for clarity's sake. Changes of scene should be numbered and underlined. Some writers (*see* Mike Walker's script on page 101) prefer a more fluid transition but note clearly when there is a change of scene.

It is usual to start a new scene on a new page. Where scenes are very short, and you hate to waste trees, just be sure to leave a clear space. When a script is going to production, the speeches within each scene are numbered on the left hand side. This is helpful for editing and direction. The director doesn't have to say to an actor; 'You know that bit in scene five where you say...'; they can simply refer to a speech number. Time is of the essence in a radio recording. Putting in the cue numbers as you write can also help if you are editing a script with the producer director. They simply have to refer to numbers where they're suggesting changes, rather than tracking down a wayward speech.

Remember that the script is read, not learnt. Don't have a speech going across pages. If a long speech starts at the bottom of page eight and continues on page nine, simply move the whole thing to page nine. If your play has long monologues extending over a couple of pages, end the page where a sentence ends then put in brackets (CONTINUED) This way the actor knows to lay out his pages so he can see two pages at a time. It helps them remember to keep momentum going.

Directions and sound effects should also be in capital letters and written in bold type or underlined. Most producers find underlining is clearer. Any directions within a speech should be in brackets, in capitals and underlined or bold:

ANNIE   I am telling you this (**COUGHS**) although you
will notice slight variations in the script layouts
throughout this book. The main thing is for actors,
producers and engineers to be able to look at the
page and see clearly and quickly what needs to be
said or done.

To make everyone really happy, however, it's best to download the BBC
template.

Studios

As soon as possible, try to see a radio play being produced. If it isn't your own,
then perhaps you have a friend with a play in production. Ask if you can sit
quietly at the back for an hour or so. This will give you a clear sense of how
engineers and actors manoeuvre round a script. All too often you'll hear an
actor ask, 'Am I doing anything while I'm saying this?' You'll hear engineers
ask; 'Are they still in the living room?' The writer hasn't made it clear enough
that characters have moved to the hall.

Simply seeing how interiors and exteriors are created with microphones
and effects helps you understand how they're used and how to write them in
to your script. You'll start to get a clearer picture of what situations work
smoothly and what scenes require a lot of unconvincing effort – usually those
crowd scenes again.

If it's your own play in production, your work isn't quite done. There will
be chances, when you hear a line is clunky, to make it better. There will be
lines you suddenly realize are superfluous. You'll hear speeches that are too
long and notice you've left characters stranded without a way to leave a
scene. You have a last chance to pass notes to the director asking to change
things.

Another essential person in the studio is the Broadcast Assistant. They
will have co-ordinated the production, tracked down agents and sent scripts
to actors, booked studios and engineers, and checked that equipment and
edit suites are available. During recording, they mark their script for takes
the director likes so they're easy to find in the edit. They do all the timings
so the director knows if a script is running long. They listen all the time for
a rustle of script that means a scene has to be re-recorded or edited around
the rustle.

Broadcast Assistants have long experience of sitting listening to play recordings – they'll notice holes in the plot or unlikely lines. I was once saved by a
Broadcast Assistant tactfully pointing out, 'This woman in scene one says this
man is sulky and taciturn but he seems to have a lot of lines, am I understanding taciturn the wrong way?' An actor was quickly deprived of half his
lines and a bad bit of writing patched over.

Your Way In

The hardest part, of course, is getting the first commission. Once this has happened, you have a friendly producer to take your next idea to, and you will have learnt a great deal in the process of getting to the broadcast of the play. The much mentioned BBC Writers Room website is one of the first ports of call for starting to write. They tell you how to submit scripts and have details of up and coming competitions or workshops. The Writers Room receives a huge number of scripts, so their process is slow but thorough.

It's very important to be bold. If you hear a play you like, listen to the end for the name of the producer. You may also hear the name of a production company or unit, such as BBC Scotland, Bristol, Manchester or Northern Ireland. This will tell you where the producer may be working. Otherwise they will probably be based at BBC Radio in London. If you really feel your script suits the style of their productions, send it to them. Producers based at the BBC, in-houseproducers, are very busy but they are always looking for new writers.

The *Radio Times* is an important magazine to have at your side. It will give you the name of the producer if you missed it. Addresses can be found in the *Writer's Handbook* (Macmillan) or *The Writers and Artists Yearbook* (A & C Black). These reference books are updated every year.

If you are from a particular area, such as Manchester, that has a regional production office, it's better to contact them directly. Part of their remit is to develop new talent in their area.

If you have a stage play in production, even it's only a rehearsed reading above a pub, invite the producer you're interested in to come along. An event makes a change from reading scripts. Of course, this doesn't show that you can write for radio but it may show that you can write drama. It could give you an opportunity to discuss your radio ideas with the producer and may move a script you send in to the top of the reading pile.

Finding the balance between being persistent and being a pest is the only way anyone gets to the first rung of the ladder.

Independents

If you heard the name of a company in the credits at the end of a play, this means it's an independent production. Independent radio production companies are listed in the *Writer's Handbook* and the *Writers' and Artists' Yearbook*. First check that they do produce drama of the type you are offering. Many of these companies have helpful websites. If you've liked a production that lists their name at the end, and feel it suits the style of your writing, write and ask if you could send a script. They may be a very small company who produce and write all the work themselves. They may not feel they can help a new writer as they produce so few dramas.

In general, independents are very accessible small companies. They are usually interested in new writers. The downside is that they only produce a percentage of the drama output. They may love your work but they have less chance of getting a production commissioned than an in-house producer. The percentage of work taken from independents varies. At the moment it is low. A good independent company, run by experienced people can offer you very valuable advice on your writing and will make every effort to sell it for you, but the odds are against them at the moment.

OTHER OUTLETS

Keep an eye on websites such as *writernet* and *4talent* for competitions. These may lead to productions or useful workshops. Workshops are often run by BBC personnel or independent producers, so you have a chance to meet people who might help. Online stations and digital stations may give you a chance to try out a short script or to write for a soap.

At the moment the BBC is the main radio drama producer, but this could change. BBC World Service drama is separate from the main drama department. It currently has limited its output to one play a month. It is a tiny department that receives submissions from all over the world so competition is tough. But it always needs fresh ideas and stories that will appeal across the globe. If you live outside the UK, it is well worth entering their International Playwrighting Competition that runs every year – see website for details.

AGENTS

If you look for agents that represent radio, there are very few. Usually they are general drama agents. If you haven't had a play on stage or anything else produced, it is unlikely that an agent will take you on to represent your first radio play. Once the play has been commissioned, then it's worth getting in touch to ask them to listen.

Radio pays so little that an agent's percentage won't feed them. They know that many radio dramatists are interesting and likely to go on to great things, but they'd prefer you to say in your covering letter that you have your radio play coming up and are writing a film script. Good drama agents will represent your whole career and introduce you to a range of radio producers, suggest you for radio series and so on – but they do feel more enthusiastic about representing you if radio isn't all that you do.

STAYING IN

Once you have had a play or two commissioned, and you have a friendly producer, you will then enter the merry dance known as the *offers round*. You have a great idea – a play about Andy Warhol trapped in a lift with an old tramp who's a defrocked priest. You want to explore Warhol's unexpectedly devout

Catholicism. You have worked out a story about their attempts to get help, escape and what happens on their final rescue. The story has many twists and turns but is essentially tense because although everyone knows Warhol didn't die trapped in a lift, your fictional, likeable tramp might die before the play ends. At this stage you won't have written the play, just mapped out the idea. Perhaps there's a Warhol anniversary or retrospective coming up – these things are worth mentioning. Perhaps your father knew Warhol, or was a defrocked priest, so you have a personal connection to the story.

What you and the producer have to create is an inspired selling document for your play. This goes in with hundreds of others and may or may not be short-listed. If it is, you have to provide a more detailed outline and add in more persuasive facts, such as how the play will sound, will there be flash-backs, will there be specially created music? This second document will be an extended version of the first. Then, you hold your breath and wait for com-mission. Then you write the play.

If it's turned down and you've worked up a head of steam about what a great idea it is, it can be very disappointing. Unless you can find a way to turn it into a stage play or approach television, you may never get to write this drama you've dreamt up.

The *offers round* system often seems unfair. It gives advantages to insiders, one could say. Then again, it gives experienced writers a chance to sustain a career in radio without wasting too much time. It means you don't have to write a whole play before you know you've been turned down.

New writers will have the whole offers round process taken care of for them by the producer; they'll pitch you as the best new writer since plays were aired and your play as stunning, unique, hilarious, etc. New writers have the advan-tage that the commissioners are looking to encourage new writers. They want to encourage established writers too, but not in a blanket way; a writer is only as good as the idea they hand in, regardless of previous success. Perhaps some writers are longstanding warhorses much trusted with adaptations and abridgements but generally, if you continue to have innovative ideas, there's a fairly even playing field once you've begun a career as a radio dramatist.

Gradually you'll build up a small network of producers you enjoy working with. Not all producers have the same tastes so your Andy Warhol play might not suit someone who you know to be a complete atheist who loathes concep-tual art. You'll develop a sense of who to approach with what idea. Sometimes they will kindly pull a face and say, 'Not for me, try Joe Angst down the corri-dor, he loves all that.'

THE SLOTS

The Single Play
Radio 4 has an afternoon play five days a week; around twenty per cent of these are by new writers. The afternoon plays are forty-five minutes long and could be about anything at all. Usually they are original drama; increasingly

they are shaking off the somewhat Home Counties feeling associated with afternoon plays. This is where new writers should aim to start. Single plays by new writers are frequently produced and give a clear indication of a writer's own voice.

There are evening plays and Saturday plays that are sixty or ninety minutes in length; new writers may gain access to these slots but the five a week, every day afternoon slot is the best to aim for. If you can show yourself able to tell a lively well-constructed story in forty-five minutes, the faster you'll find yourself with a commission.

You may have written a work of genius of seventy minutes in length, and a producer may work with you to get the piece into the right shape, but remember that people are busy. Despite the eagerness of radio producers to help new writers, they'll encourage you sooner if you seem to have grasped the existing drama structures and have a rough idea what the output is.

Listen to radio plays; it's the best way to find out how they can be structured. A good one will startle you with its economy; a bad one will leave you feeling the short forty-five minute slot was too long.

Afternoon plays can be about anything, by anyone. If you feel you are not the sort of person radio plays represent, then all the better. You and your world may not be represented because no one has written a play about them yet. The airwaves are waiting for you.

In the first six months of 2008, the subjects for afternoon plays included: events leading up to the signing of the 2005 peace treaty in Southern Sudan; a lost child; a modern version of the Sorcerer's Apprentice; Charles Dickens' life as a newspaperman; an RAF bomber pilot returning to Germany to look for forgiveness; the nineteenth-century Society for the Suppression of Vice; the Northern Rock bank crisis; the final broadcast of a pirate radio operator; Ghandi and Chaplin meeting in east London; a young man looking for love on the internet; a paparazzi photographer surprised by a celebrity; a busy househusband finding that inconveniently it may be down to him to prevent the imminent end of the world. There's comedy, tragedy, current events, history and conjecture. The plays tour through places, generations and time.

Be warned, however; producers I've interviewed have complained heartily about what they call the 'topic of the moment' play. This could be child abuse, knife crime, celebrity drug addicts – whatever's been in the news for weeks. Unless your take is unusual, heartfelt and exquisitely written, just trying to react to current events can produce a play like ten others on producers' desks.

Producers and commissioners also complain of 'gloom' and receiving far too many plays set in the past. There's nothing wrong with an historical play, but is there a contemporary resonance? Is there something in the story you feel passionate about? If you're an expert on a particular historical period or character, this may not translate into a passionate drama.

The expression 'write what you know' is often misinterpreted. You could be a housewife on a remote Scottish Island and write a good play about Algerian politics. Research gets easier and easier with the internet. What you know is

116

not the Algerian situation or culture. What you know is the characters to put in that situation, how they relate to each other and how they feel. People are all much the same the world over – just the details are different.

It is probably better to imagine what you would really like to hear in a radio play. What would you like to find out yourself? What feeling do you want to share or understand? That way the writing is honest and more likely to be compelling.

Fifteen-Minute Serial

The morning serial, sometimes called the *Woman's Hour* serial is often a dramatized reading but lively, original drama ideas that fit into the fifteen-minute slot are frequently commissioned.

The fifteen-minute slots run across five, ten and sometimes fifteen episodes. They aren't stand-alone stories unless there is a strong linking theme – stories about men in captivity; things that end up in the lost property office; people on a package holiday together. The same event viewed through the eyes of five different characters is another way to make these short drama slots relate to each other but stand alone.

The series *Ladies of Letters*, in which two middle-aged women exchange comic emails, is often cited as a good use of this slot. There was a small cast, engaging story strands and compelling characters. Very little set-up was needed – with fifteen minutes listeners need to be plunged quickly in to the story.

The budget for this slot is small and the commissions for adaptations, tend to fall to established writers. This is not the ideal slot for a first-time writer, but a strikingly original idea could squeak through on a sample script, if the fifteen-minute sample is well written and the proposal to sustain the drama over at least five short episodes is convincing. These dramas may run to more than ten episodes but usually this is for an adaptation or dramatized reading of a popular classic.

Although still called the *Woman's Hour* serial, because they immediately follow the *Woman's Hour* magazine programme, the dramas are repeated for a more general audience in the evening. They don't have to be aimed at perceived women's interests. They are unlikely to be taxing, distressing or experimental as the morning and evening slots are considered to be times when listeners are usually busy with something else – cooking or driving; or they're sitting down to relax for a moment. It's a slot for the diverting rather than mind-blowing drama.

Saturday Play

The Saturday play is sixty minutes, sometimes ninety minutes, long. This is a play of broad interest, often a detective story or comedy. It may feature well-known historical figures or significant historical events. It could be a story too grand in scale for the forty-five minute slot. It will not be too shocking or experimental as this is considered one of the few family listening slots.

Genre stories such as ghost stories, thrillers and epic love stories do well in this slot. They tend to be one-off plays but there are occasional ambitious series, such as the acclaimed adaptation of *Lord of the Rings* – experienced writer territory, definitely.

A new writer with a great story well-told could possibly get a Saturday commission. Someone suggested that this is the 'West End Play' slot. It has that feel. It's the place to find a play featuring Noel Coward as a character or an Agatha Christie adaptation. Writers have to compete with Tom Stoppard, John Mortimer, Trevor Griffiths, Alan Bennett or Charlotte Jones.

It's very hard to get your first play in the West End, almost impossible. A Saturday radio play for the talented new writer with an intriguing, broad appeal script, is more attainable. Especially if it's a comedy. As in the West End, a simple touching story can bring the crowds in as much as a gaudy musical, and second-guessing what will appeal to all is very, very difficult. It is probably safe to say that a gritty story of crack-dealing baby farmers in a burnt-out estate may not be Saturday afternoon fare.

Recent commissions have been an adaptation of *Dr No*; Patrick Barlow's version of *Joan of Arc*; *Journey into Space*; *Rebus Black and Blue* and Trevor Griffith's pair of dramas about Tom Paine.

Classic Serial

The classic serial is an adaptation that could be Edith Wharton, Jean Rhys, Thomas Mann, Joseph Heller, Chinua Achebe or Ernest Hemingway. It is a slot for the experienced, but worth studying for technique. It is possible for a successful theatre, television or film writer to be invited to adapt a book the producers feel particularly suits them, but this isn't a good route in for the completely new writer. How will you know what your voice is if you're trying to interpret Tolstoy's?

For copyright reasons, classic serials tend to be pre-1918 books. They could be history, accounts of exploration or a diary, rather than a forgotten classic novel. At this stage, there are few forgotten classic novels that haven't been hunted down by radio dramatists and producers. Anything that has been done on radio in the last ten years will not get commissioned. A popular classic with a new angle on the adaptation could be worth thinking about.

The classic serial doesn't have to be a British book of course. Is the book you're considering from a country that we see differently now and this is what makes the adaptation an interesting thing to do at the moment? Does it illustrate that the plight of a particular country or people hasn't changed in a hundred years?

Again there are complaints of gloom from the commissioners. Was everything written before 1918 a tale of woe? Are there pre-1918 comic novels where the humour is a little dated now, but an updating of the jokes could really make an entertaining production?

The Friday Play

This is a slot for modern and often experimental plays. New writing dominates here. There is a sense that people feel it's compulsory to submit gritty grim plays to the Friday slot. However, contemporary can also mean comical. It's a place for plays that make people think; that show life outside the mainstream or examine mainstream events from an unusual perspective. Real life experience is the emphasis for this slot. Usually the plays are one-offs, sixty minutes long, but a recent light-hearted five part series on the coming of Punk to suburban Britain was very successful.

This is a slot for innovative fiction drama, not biography or adaptation.

Comedy

I've said it a couple of times but it's worth saying again – coming up with a good radio sitcom will open more doors for you than if you were standing outside the BBC giving away gold bars. Well almost. Comedy is undersubscribed and overlooked by writers, but loved by radio audiences.

The morning comedy slot at eleven-thirty is usually a sitcom style drama. It usually has a comfortable quality. It could be a one off or a series. Good examples include *Cabin Pressure; Absolute Power* and *Baggage*.

Although comedies that will run and run are sought after for this slot, the episodes need to be self-contained.

There is another slot for thirty-minute comedies at six-thirty in the evening. Some of the programmes in this slot are panel shows and sketch shows. It's a time for broad, often performer-led, comedy, or comedy with a much-loved central fictional character such as *Ed Reardon's Week or Old Harry's Game*.

There are slots for late evening comedy drama at eleven o'clock. These can be fifteen- or thirty-minute episodes. They tend to be more edgy and experimental. They could be a one off, or a series. The six part series *Nebulous* is typical of the writing sought after for these slots. New sitcoms do well in the late-night slots but sketch shows and innovative formats for panel shows are also tried out here. It isn't suitable time for comic monologues, as it comes straight after the *Book at Bedtime*.

For all these comedy slots, spoofs of other radio programmes, spoof quizzes, news satire, and sitcoms set in the past or in space are the current no-nos with producers. This may simply be that they have some good ones in the pipeline or enough running already.

World Service Drama

Currently only producing one play a month, the World Service drama department is still in business. They need sixty-minute plays that will be of interest to audiences in Africa, India, Australia, Canada... Life in contemporary multicultural Britain, or an adaptation of a wide-ranging modern novel would be typical World Service commissions. There are also slots for adaptations of classic works with an international reputation.

It is important to listen to the World Service to realize how broad their sphere of interest is. Your play, even if it is light-hearted, needs to be one that tells the world something big, something universally recognizable or offering a very personal take on world events.

Recent plays include: *The Tiger's Tale*, a drama documentary marking twenty years since the first democratic uprising in Burma; a new production of Bram Stoker's *Dracula*; a dramatization of the popular 1959 novel *Zazie Dans Le Metro; Birthing Stories*, prose, poetry and documentary reflecting on what coming in to the world can mean; *Bare Brides*, a comedy about gender imbalance in China; and *To Make people Smile Again*, a drama documentary about the Spanish Civil War.

The World Service also run an annual International radio playwrighting competition for writers not normally resident in the United Kingdom, with regional prizes for writers not writing in English. Details of this is on their website, along with some useful advice on writing radio drama.

Radio 3 Drama

Radio 3 has a Sunday evening drama of ninety minutes, often a classical adaptation or a new play by an established contemporary writer – Wesker, Mamet or Stoppard, for example. New plays by new writers may be adapted for this slot if they've had a significant success at a theatre such as the Royal Court or National Theatre.

Original commissions by new writers are possible if the subject and writing are of a high standard and there is a special reason for them to be the only person to tell the story – but it is unlikely they won't have written anything before. The diary of an opposition politician in Iran may be great dramatic reading, but the diarist might need help from an experienced producer to make the piece into a radio play.

Why this diary that I've invented could make a play for Radio 3 is that it would be an event. Radio 3 needs its Sunday night dramas to be 'events' in order to tempt audiences across the dial from Radio 4, possibly Radio 2. Radio 3 has an audience that is accustomed to listening carefully. The listeners may sit and listen to a full concert of difficult music. A complicated radio play, demanding close attention, is more likely to be scheduled on Radio 3 than Radio 4. Their drama audience is not large but there is more sense that they have chosen to listen to the play rather than happened upon it while driving home.

There is a very mistaken impression that Radio 3 is all Ibsen and Shakespeare with classy casts – this is part of the output of course – but the work is often innovative, modern and humorous. As elsewhere on the radio airwaves, a good modern comedy would be welcomed on Radio 3.

Radio 3 Sunday night dramas in first six months of 2008 included: an adaptation of Douglas Coupland's novel *Girlfriend in a Coma*; a production of Tennessee Williams' *Cat on a Hot Tin Roof*; the Donmar Warehouse production of *Othello*; a modern version of Ibsen's *Enemy of the People*, set in Belfast; the 1923 expressionist classic *The Adding Machine*; a new translation of *Cyrano de*

Bergerac; a life of Marvin Gaye; the National Theatre's production of Schnizler's *Professor Berhardi*; and a life of Irish writer Flann O'Brien featuring leading Irish comedians.

The Wire

Radio 3 has an occasional experimental slot on Saturday –usually the first Saturday of every month. This Saturday slot is for new writing. Its emphasis is on a search for the unusual and experimental. This is a slot for crack-dealing baby farmer plays and things that might be deemed too shocking for an afternoon play. The shocking element can include playing with the rules of drama, occasionally playing very rough and breaking them. A Wire play can be a monologue, a comedy or a dramatic poem. Sixty minutes is the usual length.

It is a slot for writers already known to producers who want to encourage them to take a risk. It is essential listening for new writers who feel radio drama may be too full of vicars' tea parties to suit their style and preoccupations.

Recent Wire plays include *Moonmen*, Jimmy McAleavey's play about a philosophical encounter on the airwaves between an astronaut and a CB radio enthusiast in rural Ireland; *Not Talking*, Mike Bartlett's play about what happens to a relationship when it becomes impossible to talk; *My Glass Body*, an experimental monologue on infertility by Anna Furse; and *Eyewitness*, Tom Kelly's play about growing up on the brutalizing streets of Belfast.

BBC Radio 7

This digital station mostly plays archived comedy and drama material, although there are some original shows for children. Radio 7 is useful for listening to old comedies, plays and drama series that you've missed. It is a great place to immerse yourself in the form and discover how much variety it can take.

Don't Worry About All of the Above

These slots and what's required for them is liable to change. The only constant is need for the single play, forty-five or sixty minutes long, and the thirty-minute comedy drama – and people to write them.

Radio is flexible, innovative and hungry for material. It's a place to be entertaining, cutting edge, informative, or all of these. Radio is storytelling in many forms – serious, fictional, comical, truthful, urgent, salacious, moving... We never grow out of wanting to be told stories.

> I would like to be surprised and excited by new and inventive ways of telling stories. I would like to be taken on journeys to places and situations that are not the common radio fare of dysfunctional families, unhappy love affairs, and cheating husbands. I would like to see more radio scripts that really use the medium; where the writer tells his or her story in a way that is compelling because it is on radio, and that we're not listening simply to a re-vamped stage script.
>
> Gordon House, former head of BBC World Service Drama

FURTHER INFORMATION

USEFUL WEBSITES

Most important of all for new writing advice, routes in, competitions and scholarships, free downloadable templates: BBC writers room – bbc.co.uk/writersroom
See also: bbc.co.uk/worldservice
Some writing guidelines and news of radio writing opportunities: writernet.co.uk
News and radio journalism: newscript.com
Some interesting thoughts on writing radio drama from Independent radio drama producers: irdp.co.uk
Useful thoughts on writing for factual, particularly science programmes, at the website of the Association of British Science Writers: absw.org.uk
A radio station and a website full of information: channel4radio.com
And their new talent site: 4talent.com
Asian network: bbc.co.uk/asiannetwork for information on the soap *Silver Street*
The Archers, information at: bbc.co.uk/archers

ESSENTIAL PUBLICATIONS

Radio Times
Writers and Artists Yearbook (A & C Black, 2008)
Writer's Handbook (Macmillan, 2008)
Also, look in the above for independent radio production companies with websites that might prove useful.

RECOMMENDED READING

Radio Writing, a collection of essays on radio drama edited by Sam Boardman Jacobs, Seren Books.
The Crafty Art of Playmaking – Alan Aykbourn, Faber and Faber

COURSES

The Arvon Foundation run residential courses on radio writing at various times of the year. Check their website: arvonfoundation.org

INDEX OF PROGRAMMES AND SCRIPTS

INDEX OF WRITERS, PRODUCERS AND DIRECTORS